TO BELIEVE
OR
NOT BELIEVE

To Believe or Not Believe

Young Adults and the Catholic Faith

Thomas P. Rausch, SJ

Paulist Press
New York / Mahwah, NJ

Unless otherwise stated, Scripture quotations are from New Revised Standard Version Bible: Catholic Edition, copyright © 1989, 1993 National Council of the Churches of Christ in the United States of America. Used by permission. All rights reserved worldwide.

Cover image by kantver / depositphotos.com
Cover design by Sharyn Banks
Book design by Lynn Else

Copyright © 2024 by Thomas P. Rausch, SJ

All rights reserved. No part of this publication may be reproduced, stored in a retrieval system, or transmitted in any form or by any means, electronic, mechanical, photocopying, recording, scanning, or otherwise, without either the prior written permission of the Publisher, or authorization through payment of the appropriate per-copy fee to the Copyright Clearance Center, Inc., www.copyright.com. Requests to the Publisher for permission should be addressed to the Permissions Department, Paulist Press, permissions@paulistpress.com.

Library of Congress Cataloging-in-Publication Data
Names: Rausch, Thomas P., author.
Title: To believe or not believe / Thomas P. Rausch, SJ.
Description: Young adults and the Catholic faith. | New York; Mahwah, NJ: Paulist Press, [2024] | Includes index. | Summary: "This book examines the faith of young adults in the Church and the contributing cultural contexts in which they live"—Provided by publisher.
Identifiers: LCCN 2024007464 (print) | LCCN 2024007465 (ebook) | ISBN 9780809157051 (paperback) | ISBN 9780809188772 (ebook)
Subjects: LCSH: Catholic youth—Religious life.
Classification: LCC BX2355 .R34 2024 (print) | LCC BX2355 (ebook) | DDC 282.084/2—dc23/eng/20240711
LC record available at https://lccn.loc.gov/2024007464
LC ebook record available at https://lccn.loc.gov/2024007465

ISBN 978-0-8091-5705-1 (paperback)
ISBN 978-0-8091-8877-2 (e-book)

Published by Paulist Press
997 Macarthur Boulevard
Mahwah, New Jersey 07430
www.paulistpress.com

Printed and bound in the
United States of America

Fr. Lawrence E. Boadt, CSP
1942–2010
In Memoriam

Contents

Acknowledgments ix
Introduction xi
Abbreviations xvii

1. Alone in the Crowd 1
    Losing Our Youth 2
    Bowling Alone 9
    Social Media 11
    An Epidemic of Loneliness 15
    The Solitary Self 18
    Conclusion 20

2. Truth in a Post-Truth Society 23
    A Post-Truth Society 23
    Poisoned Politics 27
    An Increasing Illiteracy 30
    Disinformation 32
    Modernity's Skepticism 34
    Loss of the Humanities 38
    Truth 39
    Conclusion 41

TO BELIEVE OR NOT BELIEVE

3. Faith and Reason 43
    - Theology and Science 44
    - Interpreting the Bible 46
    - Learning from Secular Wisdom 50
    - The Problem of Suffering 55
    - Catholic Scholars and Scientists 58
    - Beyond Neo-Scholasticism 60
    - The Second Vatican Council 61
    - Theological Pluralism 62
    - Conclusion 66

4. Encountering the Divine Mystery 69
    - Signs and Wonders 70
    - God 73
    - Jesus 79
    - The Spirit 85
    - The Church 86
    - Conclusion 90

5. Jesus and Salvation 92
    - Popular Christianity 92
    - Salvation in the Jewish Scriptures 93
    - Jesus and the Kingdom/Reign of God 96
    - Understanding the Kingdom Today 100
    - Indeterminacy and Evolution 103
    - Christology 107
    - Conclusion 110

Epilogue 113

Notes 129

Index 143

Acknowledgments

THIS WORK IS HEAVILY dependent on the research of others. Among the many sources consulted, some have been particularly helpful. The Pew Research Center is a rich source of data on issues, attitudes, and communities, particularly religious ones. So is a recent report from Washington, DC's Center for Applied Research in the Apostolate (CARA), "Faith and Spiritual Life of Catholics in the United States."

James L. Heft, SM, founder of the Institute for Advanced Catholic Studies at the University of Southern California and Jan Stets, Department of Sociology at the University of California at Riverside, edited a fine collection of essays by scholars in the social sciences and humanities titled *Empty Churches: Non-affiliation in America*. Jean Twenge, professor of psychology at San Diego State University, has studied and written extensively on what she calls the "iGeneration," those super-connected young people whose lives are so much more complicated than they appear to be.

Friends and former students have shared my interest in this subject. Their encouragement was most welcome. I am especially grateful to my longtime friend and colleague Michael Downey for his careful review of the manuscript and always helpful suggestions. And to Paul McMahon at Paulist for his always careful editorial work.

Introduction

IN MY LONG YEARS of teaching, I would always begin my undergraduate classes by asking the students to write a brief religious autobiography. I would ask them to tell me something about their religious background or lack of it, images of God, religious practice, and who shaped their faith. Their responses were always diverse and often rich. They would talk about the influence of parents or mentors, often their grandparents, in handing on the faith. The responses of Mexican and Filipino students would evidence a deeply rooted Catholic culture, even if their practice might be less than regular. Others would acknowledge a need to refocus, to renew their relationship with God and their religious practice. In recent years, however, much of that has changed.

The faith that has once sustained so many and contributed so much to Western culture is in trouble today. In our secular age, many continue to depart from their churches, leaving empty spaces in the pews. Especially dramatic are the losses among our youth. More than 34 percent of those in Generation Z (born 1997–2012) are nonaffiliated. A recent study reports that the majority describe themselves as at least slightly spiritual and religious, but they disagree with the church on several issues and lack strong ties to their faith communities. Some construct their own faith, using beliefs and practices from various religious and nonreligious sources. It is not only young adult Catholics who are diminishing in number, but also teenagers.[1]

TO BELIEVE OR NOT BELIEVE

One researcher reports that, unlike their predecessors, those in Generation Z are the least likely to claim that they are "spiritual but not religious." Very often, not just church affiliation but the faith itself is gone. Explanations vary, but many are themselves children of non-practicing parents.

Recently, National Public Radio's *Morning Edition* did a weeklong series of interviews with young adults under the age of thirty.[2] Their reasons for remaining unaffiliated or leaving their religious communities tended to fall in line with several classic objections to faith such as the problem of suffering and evil, an inability to understand the symbols and stories of their religious tradition, a perceived conflict between religion and science, and disagreement with church teachings. The culture that they inhabit also has its effect, and the number continues to grow. Some social scientists forecast that before long Christians in the United States will be less than half of the population.

Our society is polarized by competing ideologies. It is often hostile to religion, particularly among its elites, and dysfunctional. A widespread social dislocation leads to the loss of an appreciation for the importance of community, not just ecclesial but also with those who promote civic and social engagement. Social media, despite its claim to bring people together, seems more often to make them more isolated, locked onto their digital screens. Rather than broadening their interests, algorithms channel their viewing to what it tracks as their interests and limits their horizons.

Young people spend hours on social media, supposedly designed to bring people together. Yet there is increasing evidence that many of them are unhappy, depressed, and isolated. The number of those considering or attempting suicide has increased considerably. Higher education does not always help. It is increasingly career oriented, with a corresponding loss of the humanities. Today, many young adult Catholics are theologically illiterate. Unfamiliar with the Catholic tradition, they see faith and science in opposition, fall into a biblical fundamentalism, or adopt theological ideas that are more cultural than Christian.

Introduction

The loss of so many young people should be a concern. Young adults have their own gifts to bring to the Church. They are open and accepting toward those who are different and bring challenges to some church positions that may need to be rethought. While often unfamiliar with the Church's rich social teachings, they are concerned about social issues and eager to be of service. They have little use for a Church that is judgmental and unwelcoming. Not a few among them feel that something is missing. As one young woman said at the end of her religious autobiography, "I wish my parents had been religious; I might have some religion myself." These are the concerns addressed in this book.

Overview

When it comes to teaching theology, Generation Z has been the most difficult. While they are not hostile and generally willing to listen, a religious background is usually missing, and they are virtually illiterate when it comes to knowledge of the Christian tradition. For Catholics especially, they know very little of the riches of that tradition, its foundations in the Scriptures, its history, its social teachings, and the principles that shape its religious imagination.

While some will admit to an idea of God that is more cultural than rooted in the Christian tradition, many seem to lack a sense of God's presence in their lives. Our gracious God promises so much more. As we pray in one of the Eucharistic Prayers, "You are indeed Holy and to be glorified, O God, who love the human race and who always walk with us on the journey of life." God's grace is all around us if we have the eyes to see. We are created for communion with the divine, and once we have sensed that presence, we begin to experience an inner emptiness that only God can fill. Ronald Rolheiser once described this as a "holy longing."[3]

I want to address young adults and those who work with them, whether as teachers, pastors, or parents. In my writing, I have always tried to address educated adults. We live today in a post-truth society with so many formed by social media rather than what we used to speak of as a liberal arts education. Disinformation is a major problem, poisoning our politics. So is the secularity of a culture that has little concern for the religious traditions that once shaped it or for the transcendent reality it presupposed. This is the world our young adults inhabit.

Evangelical Christians talk about a personal relationship with Jesus, one that he offers each one of us, but it does not happen all at once, after a word, a prayer, or a confession of faith. It begins slowly, must be nourished like any relationship, deepened, and sometimes challenged with what I call holy blasphemies—the questions we ask, the doubts that sometimes trouble us, the questions we find ourselves asking in the silence of our hearts. Can the Christian story really be true? Is God real? Does God care? Why is there so much suffering? Couldn't God show us his presence more clearly? Where do we find God in our lives?[4]

Each of our own stories are different. I had one revelatory moment that changed my life. I was just a few years from ordination when I met a lovely girl. The attraction was mutual; we came alive in each other's presence, conversation just flowed. There was a synergy in our meetings. I had to rethink what I considered my vocation and almost lost it. But on a monastic retreat, in painful confusion, I suddenly had this unmistakable conviction that the Christian story was true, that God in Jesus had indeed entered human history, that he loves us and calls us, and that he was calling me to the priesthood. I still remember this girl fondly, although we have long since lost touch. I think we all experience these minor epiphanies, moments of grace, revelations. They are moments to be cherished and to build on.

The sufferings of so many are obstacles for many to believe in a gracious creator; so is the perceived conflict between religion and science. Young adults lack examples of a transforming faith in their families, friends, and teachers. They don't always know how to recognize God's presence or discern the movements of God's Spirit. These are

Introduction

some of the issues we will consider in what follows. Although my own approach is that of a Catholic theologian, hopefully this book may be of help not just to those "raised Catholic" but to others as well.

The first chapter reviews some of the data on the disaffiliation of so many, especially young adults. It looks at the negative effects on those who spend hours on social media, and the loneliness, social dislocation, and threats to mental health that often result.

Chapter 2 explores the philosophical roots of what has become a virtually post-truth society, and how it has poisoned our politics and civic life, spread disinformation through the abuse of social media, and resulted in an increasing illiteracy. An impoverished theory of knowing has led to a loss of transcendence. In their efforts to prepare students for their careers, our colleges and universities have given up the pursuit of wisdom through the humanities. The chapter then considers how truth itself might be understood.

The third chapter addresses the traditional Catholic principle on the complementarity of faith and reason, seeing them as different ways of knowing. A commitment to this principle determines how Catholics approach the interpretation of the Scriptures. It offers some insight into the problem of suffering, even if it remains a mystery, and how it has encouraged a long history of Catholic scholars who have made major contributions to the sciences. Finally, the chapter considers how Catholic theology has changed in recent times, particularly under the influence of the Second Vatican Council.

Titled "Encountering the Divine Mystery," chapter 4 considers the origins of Christian faith not with a doctrine or a message but with a transforming encounter with the person of Jesus. It warns about a distracting emphasis on the supernatural or the dramatic, on "signs and wonders," and points to ways the divine mystery we confess as Father, Son, and Holy Spirit is disclosed in our experience, which then leads to a consideration of the Church.

Chapter 5 reviews the doctrine of salvation, beginning with a critique of the individualist notion of salvation so widespread in popular

TO BELIEVE OR NOT BELIEVE

U.S. culture. It traces salvation through its origins in the Jewish Scriptures, the notion of the kingdom of God in the preaching of Jesus, and how we might understand it today. As God's salvific work is ongoing, it looks at God's agency hidden within the evolutionary process. It also briefly considers Christology.

The epilogue offers some concluding reflections.

Abbreviations

Documents of Vatican II

DV *Dei Verbum*: Dogmatic Constitution on Divine Revelation

GS *Gaudium et Spes*: Pastoral Constitution on the Church in the Modern World

LG *Lumen Gentium*: Dogmatic Constitution on the Church

Pope Francis

AL *Amoris Laetitia*: The Joy of Love

EG *Evangelii Gaudium*: The Joy of the Gospel

FT *Fratelli Tutti*: All Brothers: On Fraternity and Social Friendship

LS *Laudato Si'*: On Care for Our Common Home

1

Alone in the Crowd

IN RECENT DECADES, the religious demographics of the United States have changed considerably. As Christian churches continue to experience the hemorrhaging of their members, social scientists are predicting that Christians will soon make up less than half of the U.S. population. In the early 1970s, a considerable majority of Americans claimed to be Christian, some 89 percent. By 2019, however, that number had dropped to 65 to 70 percent of American adults, depending on the survey. Of these, 43 percent identify as Protestants, but that number would drop considerably if born-again and evangelicals Christians were separated from the group. Some 25 percent of Protestants identify as born-again/evangelical, while only 18 percent belong to the mainline churches. The number of white evangelicals dropped from 19 percent to 16 percent in 2019. Most confessional churches are declining dramatically.

Catholic losses also have been significant, dropping from 23 to 20 percent of the U.S. population. A 2011 Pew Research Center study said that almost one in three of those raised Catholic have left the Church. The greatest losses have been in the Northeast, where 36 percent identified as Catholics in 2009, compared to 27 percent today.[1] The number of Hispanic Catholics is also declining. Another Pew Center study shows that the percentage of Hispanics who identify as Catholics has dropped from 67 percent in 2010 to 43 percent as of 2022, a significant loss.[2] Some will move to evangelical communities that promise them "a personal relationship with Jesus," though that number too is diminishing. In terms of attendance at Mass, white Catholics attending at least a couple of times a year has dropped from 73 percent in 2019 to 45 percent in 2022. Hispanic attendance has also declined in the same period from 65 to 47 percent.[3]

Losing Our Youth

Losses among young people are particularly significant. The departure of middle-class youth from their church began in the late sixties and seventies and has continued to increase significantly. In a largely secular culture and a society whose elites are not generally friendly toward religion, the number of the religiously unaffiliated, especially among young people, continues to rise.

I wrote about this more than fifteen years ago, exploring the religious individualism and tendency of so many young people to construct their own religious identities, their loss of ecclesial faith, "thin" commitment to the institutional church, and lack of familiarity with the stories, root metaphors, and doctrines of the Christian tradition. There was considerable evidence emerging. A 2000 study from Georgetown's Center for Applied Research in the Apostolate (CARA) noted that only 21 percent of young adults attended Mass every week or more.[4] Another important 2005 study by Christian Smith and Melinda Lundquist Denton reported that "U.S Catholic teenagers are behind their Protestant peers—sometimes by as much as 25 percentage points—when measured by several standards of religious belief, practice, experience, and commitments."[5]

Two decades later, the situation is much worse. The number of adults among the "nones," those who answer "none" when asked what church or religious tradition they belong to, has continued to grow. Among the young people who make up the postmillennial generation, usually called Generation Z (1997–2012), 34 percent are religiously unaffiliated. They are the least religious, as compared to 29 percent among the millennials (1981–86) and 25 percent in Generation X (1965–80).[6] Reports in terms of gender are mixed; some see disaffiliation higher among men, others don't find significant differences. Departures are higher among the less educated.

Among young Latinos born in the United States between the ages of eighteen and twenty-nine, about half, 49 percent, identify as religiously nonaffiliated,[7] although Allan Deck reports that 43 percent of respondents to a CARA survey give as reason for their infrequent practice that "they are not very religious and/*or prefer practicing their faith outside the parish*," rooting this historically, not in traditional, diocesan parishes with Sunday Mass but in domestic religion and popular Catholicism.[8] *Christianity Today* reports that the "nones" are growing even among Black Americans.

A 2020 CARA national survey reported that of 13 percent of young adult Catholics who attended Mass at least once a week before the COVID-19 pandemic, predictions are that almost one-third will attend less frequently afterward.[9] It is also true that many young Catholics who participate in well-prepared campus liturgies during their college years drop out after they graduate, and it is not certain if they will later return. If nothing else, it suggests the need for better liturgies.

Jean Twenge, in a book on Gen Z, which she identifies as the iGen because they arose at a similar time when iPhones became so widely used, says that the younger generations are disassociating not just from religious institutions but from religion entirely, even at home and in their hearts. She argues that they are the least likely to claim that they are "spiritual but not religious," a break with older millennials.[10] Regardless, not all Gen Zers are alike. While many are turned off by institutional religion, and thus don't see themselves as religious, they are looking for spiritual meaning in their lives. And they hunger for a community in which they are loved and supported, even a community with meaningful rituals.

In an important book on this phenomenon, James Heft notes that some young adults are "hard-wired" with a religious sensibility; they are able to combine the secular and religious dimensions of their lives.[11] Two other researchers report that lapsed Catholics were very likely to believe in God; more than three-quarters claimed that religion was important to them and about 40 percent continued to pray daily.[12] Some researchers refer to them as a neglected group, those lapsed Catholics who still identify as Catholics but rarely attend church services. Sometimes described as "liminal nones," they are halfway between secular and religious in their identities. They constitute half or even more of the nones.[13]

Explanations for the loss of so many of our young people are varied. A 2017 study by Saint Mary's Press says that 74 percent of Catholics who leave the church do so between the ages of ten and twenty, pointing to *three* categories of disaffiliation. "The injured" point to negative experiences like the death of a loved one, a divorce, or long-term illness that disrupts their lives. "The drifters" ultimately drop out because of lack of engagement with a faith community or support from family or peers. "The dissenters" are those who disagree with church teachings on issues like same-sex marriage, birth control, or abortion, although many who oppose abortion also support a woman's right to choose.[14]

The move to the extreme right by churches heavily invested in the culture wars should not be discounted as a cause. It is significant. Some conservative Protestants object to their churches demonizing LGBTQ people, their failure to address white racism, or their inability to move beyond right-wing extremism and Donald Trump.[15] One study of "dechurched" mainline and Catholic Christians found them far less likely than evangelicals to embrace the "prosperity Gospel" (31 versus 58 percent) or Christian nationalism (20 to 29 percent).[16] Many young Catholics object to their church's unwillingness to welcome gay members and fully include women in its life and ministry. With the resulting polarization in our society and our churches, Brett Hoover suggests that religious identity risks being divorced from actual religion. "The marriage of Evangelicalism with Republican conservatism (which extended to many churchgoing white Catholics) eventually became so seamless that religious identity seems increasingly articulated in terms of partisan policies."[17]

Some scholars point to the religious illiteracy of so many young adults today as a significant factor. John Cavadini from the University of Notre Dame argues that young adults are ignorant of the basic terminology of the faith and calls for a renewed pedagogy of the basics. Cathleen Kaveny points to a catechesis focused more on engaging their emotions than challenging their intellects, leaving them without an in-the-bones sense of Catholic identity. Mark Poorman says that many Catholic students at Notre Dame seem unaware of basic theological distinctions among Christian traditions and between Christianity and other religions.[18]

Other scholars point to an impoverished religious imagination. The University of Notre Dame's *Church Life Journal* rejects the traditional argument about inadequate catechesis leading to a loss of faith. This assumes that people choose their actions and identity based primarily on theological beliefs:

> Yet this widely held assumption has come under fire recently. James K. A. Smith's work on cultural liturgies draws on Augustine, cognitive psychology, and philosophies of action to challenge this myth: people's behavior is not driven primarily by what they know and believe but by what they love and imagine as good. This is not to say that beliefs are unimportant, but that what gives shape to human action is primarily one's imagination and enduring dispositions (*habitus*) rather than mere assent to doctrine.[19]

Christian life is certainly more than catechesis, doctrine, and rules. It is important to find ways to communicate something of the beauty of the Catholic tradition and how life in Christ satisfies our deepest longings. As Pope Benedict XVI says at the beginning of his encyclical, *Deus Caritas Est*, "Being Christian is not the result of an ethical choice or a lofty idea, but the encounter with an event, a person, which gives life a new horizon and a decisive direction. Saint John's Gospel describes that event in these words: 'God so loved the world that he gave his only Son, that whoever believes in him should...have eternal life'" (no. 1). Pope Francis uses similar language.

Perhaps the most significant explanation for today's unchurched youth is that so many are the children of nonpracticing parents. According to The Survey Center on American Life, "The parents of millennials and Generation Z did less to encourage regular participation in formal worship services and model religious behaviors in their children than had previous generations. Many childhood religious activities that were once common, such as saying grace, have become more of the exception than the norm."[20] Smith and Denton argue that "the evidence clearly shows that the single most important social influence on the religious and spiritual lives of adolescents is their parents."[21] Jean Twenge points out that teens with college-educated fathers were *more* likely to attend religious services than those without.[22]

The pervasive individualism of American society is another significant factor. That individualism is deeply rooted in both the history of the United States and its resulting culture. Robert Neelly Bellah attributes it to the dominance of Protestantism in the country's past. The country was founded by dissenting Protestants, sectarians often persecuted by established churches in their countries of origin; they consequently exalted freedom of conscience against established authorities, whether political, ecclesial, or patriarchal, and tended to question all authoritative voices. Such a religious individualism frequently leads to a subjective approach to religion, with young people especially finding the sacred outside of religious institutions, exalting experience at the expense of religious authority.[23] This, however, suggests a religion based on subjective tastes, not one rooted in anything real or historical, or rooted in any objective order or truth.

Bellah also points to the Protestant "near exclusive focus on the relation between Jesus and the individual, where accepting Jesus Christ as one's personal Lord and Savior becomes almost the whole of piety." He reports some of those interviewed for his book, *Habits of the Heart*, who claim that "if I'm all right with Jesus, then I don't need the church."[24] Two evangelicals make a similar point. According to Scot McKnight, much of evangelicalism focuses not on Jesus and the kingdom of God but on Paul and his doctrine of justification by faith.

Similarly, Michael Gerson, a former speech writer for George W. Bush, writes, "Evangelicals often think that being a Christian means the individualistic acceptance of Jesus as their personal Savior. But this is quite different from following the example of Jesus we find in the Gospels."[25] This reduces Christianity to a religion of salvation, privatizing piety and too often overlooking the social and ethical dimensions of the Gospel. Jesus calls men and women to discipleship, accompanying him in his historical ministry and continued in his body, the Church.

A recent study by Stephen Bullivant, *Nonverts: The Making of Ex-Christian America*, uses the rather difficult term *nonverts* to describe those raised in a religious tradition but later abandoning it, joining the nones. For an explanation, he points to changes in American political, social, and family life that reshaped fundamental attitudes toward faith and religious belonging, among them, the end of the struggle against "godless communism," to be replaced by a new struggle against religious extremism, especially Islamic terrorism, a growing secular culture both here and abroad that introduced a chasm between traditional religious values and popular culture, the fact that so many children grew up in homes with parents who practiced their religious faith rarely if at all, the popularity of the New Atheists, and most of all the internet. Calling attention to the negative influence of the internet is significant. He cites the work of Paul McClure, who uses survey data to illustrate its significant influence on the loss of faith, arguing that "the more time one spends on the Internet, the greater the odds are that an individual can be predicted to be religiously unaffiliated."[26]

Smith and Denton coined the term *moralistic therapeutic deism* to describe the subjective image of God emerging from their research on teenagers, but they also suggest that it may well be the dominant faith of our culturally post-Christian, individualistic society. It presumes a God who created and ordered the world, wants people to be nice and fair to each other, and be happy and feel good about themselves, but does not need to be particularly involved in their lives unless needed to resolve a problem.[27] A later article carries his analysis further. From its perspective, being moral doesn't mean much more than being "kind, nice, pleasant, courteous, responsible, at work on improving oneself, taking care of one's health, and doing one's best to be successful." God is not personally involved and remains at a safe distance. This is not a God of grace and forgiveness, a trinitarian God whose Son entered time as Jesus of Nazareth and dwells in our hearts.[28]

In my later teaching years, I've found another common quasi-religious vision. Most frequently students would say something about "believing in a higher power." But what that meant for most was quite different from the higher power appealed to as an aid to transformation in Alcoholics Anonymous groups. What my students were referring to was usually vague and undefined, much like "the Force" in *Star Wars*. They had little to say in response when I would ask, is this higher power personal? Do you have a relationship with it? Does it love you? Is it just a feeling? Still, belief in a higher power suggests an openness to the divine.

The individualism of contemporary society often leaves many young adults isolated, disconnected from sustaining relationships or traditions, and thrown back on themselves for their values, beliefs, or standards. Their families are often dysfunctional. Their civic or social relationships are limited. Few belong to church communities that nurture not just faith but social responsibility and altruism. Churches connect us to God and to each other. Pastors and theologians argue that a spirituality that does not connect us to others is not an authentic spirituality. This loss of faith and social isolation has not passed unnoticed by social observers.

Bowling Alone

One of the first to call attention to this lost sense of community and social dislocation on the part of so many was political scientist Robert Putnam, first in an article (1995) and then in a book (2000) with the striking title "Bowling Alone."[29] Bowling is essentially a social sport. No one bowls alone, but the image is a fitting metaphor for so many of our youth today. Putnam notes how the post–World War II generation responded to President John F. Kennedy's challenge to pick up the torch of leadership. There was a sense that civic life would be enhanced by talk about a "participatory democracy," even if limited by issues of race and gender. Still, people were linked by a network of relationships called "social capital" by the social scientists.

By the late 1980s and '90s, people began talking about breakdown of community, with a lack of social connections and civic engagement. As fewer people read newspapers or watched the news on television, people became increasingly less informed. The number of those voting also dropped. While engagement in civil life diminished significantly, so did Americans' ability to trust their neighbors. "In 1996 only 8 percent of all Americans said that 'the honesty and integrity of the average American' were improving, as compared with 50 percent of us who thought we were becoming less trustworthy."[30]

Americans have long been considered a religious people. Many of the first colonists were fleeing religious persecution; those who followed them were known for their high levels of participation in churches or synagogues. As Putnam argues, religious engagement has long been closely associated with other forms of civic involvement, with 75 to 80 percent of church members giving to charity, as opposed to only 55 to 60 percent of nonmembers, and 55 to 60 percent volunteering, as opposed to only 30 to 35 percent of nonmembers. Their churches were generally institutional providers of social services, rooted both in a shared faith and in their social connectedness.[31]

Putnam traces similar losses in social capital in the workplace, less formal social connections like informal gatherings of neighbors and friends or less civic engagement such as philanthropy and volunteering for community service. David Campbell sees the data about civic involvement by those in religious congregations as suggesting that "as people pull away from religion, they retreat from civic life."[32]

Robert Wuthnow, a sociologist who has long observed religion in America, echoes many of Putnam's findings. He writes about a loss of a sense of community, social connections, and an increasing isolation in contemporary American society. Fewer than half of those in his surveys believe that their fellow citizens genuinely care about others. There is a greater focus on the self. As the number of self-help groups or 12-step programs continues to grow, membership in traditional organizations such as the League of Women Voters, Lions Clubs, volunteer fire-fighting departments, Red Cross volunteers, NAACP, the Sierra Club, and Boy Scouts and Girl Scouts continues to drop. Some studies show Americans involved in a range of civic and social activities, but often those that require little in terms of commitment.

With lack of communal ties, social networks, and activities, many find it difficult to pass on their moral values to their children. Connections today are loose, institutions porous, and informational technologies complex. More and more people are becoming isolated, lacking sustaining social relationships. "Loose connections tempt citizens to behave in a less civil manner because relationships are more likely to be transitory and casual than enduring and dependent on good will."[33]

Family life is also in trouble, with fewer marriages staying together. The number of marriages ending in divorce varies between 40 and 50 percent, while the number of couples cohabiting continues to rise. For Catholics especially, a sacramental sense of marriage is diminishing. In the United States, the number of Catholic marriages between 1970 and 2020 dropped from 420,000 to 131,000, while petitions for annulments dropped from a high of 72,308 in 1990 to 19,500 initiated in 2019; although, of course, fewer marriages means fewer petitions for annulments.[34] This suggests that fewer Catholic are marrying in the church or taking advantage of the annulment process. They are also having fewer children; about 62 percent of all adult Catholics live without a child in their households. As one cynic commented, with some truth, young adults are raising dogs, not children.

With the increasing number of divorces, fewer marriages, and the number of children born outside of marriage, by 2022 almost one quarter of children in the United States were living with a single parent, a number higher than in any other country in the world! Also rising are the number of adults living alone—28 percent of U.S. households in 2021, according to the Census Bureau—and the number of unhoused people. These statistics suggest an increasing isolation of many today.

Social Media

If young people today are often disconnected from family and church, they are rarely disconnected from their social media platforms. A 2022 Pew Research Center study reports that their social media usage is up from 92 percent in 2014–15 to 97 percent in 2022. Some 95 percent of U.S. teens have digital devices such as smartphones, 90 percent use desktop or laptop computers, and 80 percent use gaming consoles. Some 97 percent of teens say that they use the internet daily, and 46 percent use it almost constantly, up 24 percent from 2014 2015. Black and Hispanic teens report being on the internet almost constantly, compared to 37 percent for white teens.[35]

The platforms favored by young people continue to change. Facebook, once highly popular, has dropped from 71 percent in 2014–15 to 32 percent today, although it is still widely used by adults. Leading platforms today include YouTube, TikTok, Instagram, and Snapchat. Some 86 percent of teenage TikTok or Snapchat users say that they access those platforms daily. The 51 percent of teens almost constantly online, not just on social media, acknowledge that they spend too much time on those sites, while only 26 percent of those online several times per day say they visit social media too often.[36] Some studies indicate that teens spend five to six hours per day on new media sites.[37]

While more research is needed on how social media usage affects young people, there are already signs that raise concerns. One study found that Instagram has a harmful effect on the body images of some teenage girls. Some engage in unhealthy practices such as "sexting," sending indecent pictures of themselves to others, leaving themselves vulnerable to blackmail. Others become self-obsessed and narcissistic, posting hundreds of images of themselves performing or posing in revealing costumes on TikTok, or measuring their worth by the number of "likes" their postings receive.

TikTok may also be influencing our sexual mores by encouraging sexual experimentation. It posts numerous videos of scantily clad, beautiful young people kissing intimately—boy and girl, boy and boy, girl and girl—without any sense of sexual responsibility. Instagram posts are often explicitly sexual in content.

As Twenge argues, the attitudes of teens toward sex have changed, even for those who are religious. They are more likely to see nothing wrong with various sexual relations, even though they may not engage in them themselves. Regardless, the number of women who have had sex with at least one other woman has tripled since the early 1990s and millennial and iGen women are much more likely than their predecessors to have had sex with another woman. Bisexual relations are also much more frequent. The large increase in bisexual experience suggests that many today are having sex with both men and women without necessarily identifying as gay, lesbian, or bisexual.[38] The discovery of online communities with special interest can challenge a person's religious commitment that is already being threatened by an enveloping secular culture.

Social scientists point to young people becoming addicted to their social media platforms, limiting their information or their relationships to what they find there. While there are some positive benefits, among them rapid access to information, becoming rapid decision-makers, and improving visual skills, the less positive benefits are more limited attention spans and an inability to concentrate or allow time for critical thinking and analysis. Some research suggests that heavy social media use causes changes in brain structure, affecting learning and memory.[39] In 2021, Chinese authorities limited minors in China playing online games to one hour a day. In March 2023, TikTok said it would limit users under eighteen years of age to sixty minutes per day. In part, this was due to a growing concern from governments about security and the tendency to push certain posts.

The amount of time that young people spend playing video games—97 percent of those between twelve and seventeen years old—is a serious problem. Nicholas Kardaras argues that in a cold and mechanistic world stripped of its myths, video games can provide a virtual world of fantasy and dangerous adventure. With heavy use, kids who are alienated or socially isolated find these "digital drugs" as addictive as others find heroin, with onscreen virtual gunfire in games like *World of Warcraft* supplying a similar release of dopamine. Some have difficulty distinguishing the virtual world of the game from real life. Kardaras cites "a 2016 brain-imaging study published in the journal *Molecular Psychiatry* in which video games were found to affect the development of microstructural properties of the brain associated with negative psychological outcomes."[40]

Some longtime users show diminished social skills, difficulty maintaining eye contact, or recognizing nonverbal cues in conversation. Twenge cites evidence that young adults are in many ways less social. The number of teens who "hang out" with their friends every day in the last fifteen years has been reduced by half. They also go out less frequently with their friends, spending less face-to-face time with peers than any previous generation and spending far less time at malls as teens did in the 1980s and '90s. College students also spend less time together.[41] She cites studies showing that "teens who spend more time on social media are more likely to value individualistic attitudes and less likely to value community involvement."[42]

I often see a couple at a table in a restaurant on their cell phones rather than talking to each other. When I walk around the campus at night, I notice many students with their faces illuminated by their mobile devices. Others slow down traffic, crossing the street slowly with their eyes on their smart phones. In a recent interview with three high school students, I learned that each spent at least two hours a day on social media. In China, I found students popping open their phones as soon as the class ended.

Social media was supposed to bring people together, establishing networks of friends stretching across countries and continents. All too often, however, social media has not created understanding and community but division, polarizing relationships in society, government, even the church. Some platforms host critical comments, even insults. Social media's contribution to what is emerging as a post-truth society has been enormous. More on this later.

For many young people, the impact of social media has been detrimental. Some are victims of online bullying or sexual exploitation. Narcissistic showmanship is not unusual. Others boast of hundreds of online friends, but those are usually virtual friends, not real ones. Many young people admit that they are terribly lonely.

Pope Francis is aware of the seductive, addictive character of social media. In *Fratelli Tutti* (Brothers All), he warned about social media platforms spreading prejudice and hate (no. 45). As he said in an "An Address to Young People during the Synod":

> You are priceless! You are not up for sale! Please, do not let yourselves be bought. Do not let yourselves be seduced. Do not let yourselves be enslaved by forms of ideological colonization that put ideas in your heads, with the result that you end up becoming slaves, addicts, failures in life. You are priceless. You must repeat this always: I am not up for sale; I do not have a price. I am free! Fall in love with this freedom, which is what Jesus offers.[43]

An Epidemic of Loneliness

According to a survey published by Cigna in 2020, more than three in five Americans are lonely, with more and more reporting feelings of being poorly understood, left out, and lacking companionship. Since the survey was first conducted in 2018, the number of those reporting such symptoms has risen by 13 percent. According to one researcher, 15 percent of American men report having no close friends, an increase from 3 percent in 1990. Another study from the Center for Disease Control (CDC) found that from 2009 to 2021, the share of American high school students who report "persistent feelings of sadness or hopelessness" rose from 26 percent to 44 percent.[44] Feelings of isolation were highest among Generation Z, young adults between the ages of eighteen and twenty-two years. Loneliness was more common among heavy users of social media, compared to light users.

Cigna reported that pervasive loneliness affects not just mental health, leading to anxiety and depression, but also physical health.[45] New trend data from the CDC's Youth Risk Behavior

Survey published early in 2023 was alarming. It reported that there was a decrease in risky behaviors, including risky sexual behaviors, substance abuse, and bullying at school, but other indicators had worsened significantly, among them unprotected sex, expressions of violence, and fear of going to school because of safety concerns, with more than 40 percent of high school students with feelings of sadness or hopelessness, as well as an increase in students considering or attempting suicide. Teen girls and LGBTQ teens especially are experiencing extremely high levels of mental distress, violence, and substance use. The number of girls who reported they seriously considered suicide in 2021 was up 19 percent from a decade ago. Alcohol use is also higher among girls than boys.[46] Suicide is the second most common cause of death for young adults in the United States.

More and more studies describe this increase in loneliness as an epidemic. According to the Institute for Family Studies, young adults today are experiencing loneliness, social isolation, and disconnection. Researchers point to various causes; the heavy use of social media and the isolation brought on by the COVID-19 pandemic also delayed family formation. Those in Generation Z point to a feeling of loneliness when they were growing up; an increasing number were raised in single parent households, or by divorced parents (52 percent), or in smaller families, and are marrying later.[47]

Although Twenge is careful to examine other possible causes, she points to the heavy use of smartphones as the most likely cause for the unhappiness experienced by so many teenagers and college students. As the use of smartphones spread, in-person interactions plummeted, with an increase in feelings of loneliness, exclusion, anxiety, and depression. Girls, who spend far more time on social media than boys, reported significantly higher levels of such feelings. Posting selfies and comparing them to perfect pictures of other girls, seemingly spontaneous but actually carefully constructed, has magnified body image problems. The number of teens cutting themselves and discussing it on social media also increased significantly.

One mother discovered that her daughter had seventeen Facebook accounts.

Nor are girls the only ones affected. Depression among young people from all ethnic groups, socioeconomic classes, and different parts of the country has skyrocketed. One survey showed that 56 percent more teens experienced a major depressive episode in 2015 than in 2010, and 60 percent experienced more severe impairment. Loss of sleep also affects the health and mood of young people. Teens should get at least nine hours of sleep a night, but many now sleep less than seven because of time spent on their electronic devices, especially those who use them before trying to go to sleep. As noted earlier, the number of those considering suicide has also increased significantly.[48]

An article in *Psychology Today* argues that a connected world paradoxically leaves many feeling disconnected; 73 percent of Generation Z report feeling alone either sometimes or always—the highest level of any generation. These feelings are leading to mental health issues that are beginning to impact the workplace; 75 percent of Generation Z and half of Millennials left a job because of mental health reasons, compared with 34 percent of other generations. The article points to three causes. One is overstimulation. Distractions from work, social media, activities, and future commitments eat up our cognitive resources, leaving little time to focus on others as we choose the impersonal over the personal. Another cause is social media itself. Heavy users are significantly more likely to feel isolated, left out, and without companionship, as we have seen. Social media can easily lead to unhealthy comparisons with others who present only their best sides, although one researcher argues that it can work against loneliness for those who are highly social.

A third cause is described as a "dependency shift," with information decentralized, no longer coming from family, neighbors, or coworkers, that is from our human relationships, but from Google, YouTube, artificial intelligence, or other online sources accessed individually.[49] An increasing number of people rely on these sources, rather than print and digital sources. Newspapers are shutting down—in 2020, at a rate of two per week—leaving an increasing number of people dependent on social media sources that often lack expert opinion or critical analysis.

The Solitary Self

The biblical story of the creation of man and woman includes the importance of companionship: "The LORD God said, 'It is not good that the man should be alone'" (Gen 2:18). Social isolation is neither healthy nor spiritually fulfilling. We are not meant to live disconnected lives. Few offspring are as dependent on others as those of the human. The infant reaches out instinctively for its mother's breast. It needs not just nourishment but care, tender touch, and relationships if it is to develop a positive self-image and sense of identity. Without other people, language ability does not develop and, without language, self-consciousness. To be human is to be in relationship with others.

This need for contact, for a relationship suggests the need for community. Pope Francis has stressed the interconnectedness of all creatures. In his poetic encyclical *Laudato Si'*, he says that "it cannot be stressed enough that everything is interconnected. Time and space are not independent of one another, and not even atoms or subatomic particles can be considered in isolation.... A good part of our genetic code is shared by many living beings" (no. 138). It is precisely this interrelatedness of microscopic infrastructures, plant and animal life, and weather systems that constitutes an ecosystem. Of course, human activity plays a crucial role in the encyclical's basic point that as human beings we belong to one single human family, dependent on each other and on the earth that is our common home.

But as Francis writes in his social encyclical *Fratelli Tutti*, "In today's world, the sense of belonging to a single human family is fading, and the dream of working together for justice and peace seems an outdated utopia" (no. 30). Society is increasingly fragmented and polarized. In the United States, Blue states are divided from Red, and Congress is scarcely able to govern. The culture wars are still being waged. Southern Republicans continue to challenge LGBTQ rights; pass legislation that threatens voter rights (especially for people of color); remove books from public schools; and in the guise of rejecting Critical Race Theory, ignore America's long history of racial prejudice and violence. Democrats insist on enforcing social policy regarding sex and gender, untethered from traditional norms of morality. Abortion remains a polarizing issue, with little effort to work out a compromise that meets the concerns of both sides. Churches argue that their religious liberty is under threat.

Francis frequently calls attention to different obstacles to a sense for our common humanity. Among them, a "throw-away" world in which persons are no longer seen as a paramount value, an insufficient respect for human rights, the loss of a sense of mutual responsibility on which civil society is based, and populist regimes blocking immigrants from entering their countries. Especially damaging is racism, which in Francis's words, is like a virus that mutates and goes into hiding, only to lurk in waiting (no. 97). He also raises concerns about digital media that, rather than building bridges, can block the development of authentic interpersonal relationships, which take time and careful cultivation.

Reflecting on the parable of the good Samaritan in *Fratelli Tutti*, he calls attention to the priest and a Levite, two religious men who pass by the victim of the robbers on the road to Jericho without stopping to assist him. His comment on the passage: "It shows that belief in God and the worship of God are not enough to ensure that we are actually living in a way pleasing to God" (no. 74). What reigns instead is a cool, comfortable and globalized indifference, born of deep disillusionment concealed behind a deceptive illusion: thinking that we are all powerful, while failing to realize that we are all in the same boat" (no. 30).

Conclusion

The Canadian philosopher Charles Taylor sees the roots of modern secularism stretching back to the Reformation, with its stripping the enchanted medieval cosmos of its mystery, its narratives of faith and religious practice, and ultimately its eschatological hope, replacing it with an emphasis on personal faith.[50] The increasing disconnection of so many today from their churches and even from their Christian faith, especially the young and many still in their teenage years, may be one of the fruits of a pervasive secularism. Some young people no longer even identify with the claim, "I'm spiritual but not religious." Some subscribe to a cultural idea of the divine who is there when needed but makes no demands, a God that has little to do with historic Christianity. Many young adults are also disconnected from each other. Some speak of an epidemic of loneliness. We all need friends and companions to flourish.

The explanations for the contemporary loss of faith are many. Not only has American culture become increasingly secular, with fewer institutional supports for religious practice, but many young people, growing up in nonreligious homes, have been alienated from their religious communities, dropping out of their churches because of differences between what they value and what their churches or communities teach. They often report finding their churches too judgmental. Clergy sexual abuse has also alienated many Catholics.

Evangelicals were more likely to be involved in their congregations, but less likely involved in the broader community; however, more recent studies show similar losses even here. Many young Catholics object to their church's inability to welcome their peers who belong to the LGBTQ community; Jean Twenge calls this antigay attitude the elephant in the room.[51] They also criticize the church's failure to acknowledge and incorporate fully the gifts of women. They have little patience with ecclesial intolerance, but it is also true that many young people exhibit a lack of familiarity with the basic truths of Christianity, for religious illiteracy is widespread.

The internet is a rich resource with so much information only a click away; it can be used for educational purposes, but it can also result in an information overload, offering multiple and conflicting narratives, visions, and beliefs. Social media platforms use artificial intelligence to track viewers' interests and reinforce them, which can close viewers off to wider issues. The constant celebration of youth and beauty can also lead young people to harmful comparisons, leading to depression and a lack of self-worth. Self-care and identity construction is important to them. Many have hundreds of virtual friends but few real ones. They are hungry for meaning, but some are searching for it in all the wrong places.[52]

I do not mean to suggest that all young people are self-obsessed, wrapped up in themselves and closed to others. In my long years of teaching, I have found many of our youth have a generosity of spirit; they are accepting of those who are different and eager to be of service.

In his apostolic letter *Amoris Laetitia* (The Joy of Love), Pope Francis asks that those in "irregular situations" receive not condemnation but accompaniment, pastoral care, and discernment. He appeals to the "law of gradualness" (no. 295), behind which lies Jesus's way of compassion and mercy, not harsh judgments that overlook the complexity of different situations and so often drive young people from the church.

So, how do we show young people the way of Jesus? How do we help others to discover the God whose mystery we often sense, who reveals his presence in moments of quiet and contemplation? This God is not distant, beyond our reach. The God who made the heavens and the earth also fashioned our hearts and dwells there, giving us a share in the light, communion, and love that is the divine life. We are made for communion with others: "Each of us is fully a person when we are part of a people" (FT 182).

As Pope Francis says in *Evangelii Gaudium*, if we succeed in expressing adequately and with beauty the essential content of the Gospel, surely this message will speak to the deepest yearnings of people's hearts (no. 265). His emphasis on beauty is important; beauty draws us toward the divine. For our young people especially, we must aim at more than their heads; our evangelization and catechesis have to find ways to touch them affectively, to find the way to their hearts.

2
Truth in a Post-Truth Society

CHRISTIANITY HAS LONG prized truth; it is both an attribute of the divine and the goal of our knowing. Metaphysically, truth is included among the transcendentals—the one, good, true, and beautiful. Thomas Aquinas (1225–74) generally listed three: unity or oneness (*unum*), truth (*verum*), and goodness (*bonum*), while later theologians added beauty (*pulchrum*) to the list. The transcendentals are understood as properties of the divine, but we also feel drawn toward them, and thus toward God. According to the *Catechism of the Catholic Church*, "All creatures bear a certain resemblance to God, most especially man, created in the image and likeness of God. The manifold perfections of creatures—their truth, their goodness, their beauty—all reflect the infinite perfection of God" (no. 41).

A Post-Truth Society

Yet if truth is honored in the Catholic tradition, today it is under threat. Social commentators frequently speak of a "post-truth society." Moisés Naím defines post-truth as "a frontal attack on our shared sense of reality."[1] Wikipedia traces the term to concerns regarding claims of public truth that mushroomed after the 2016 U.S. presidential election, but a certain fragility to the concept of truth was already evident long before the political battles of the twenty-first century. Under the influence of modernity, the process of knowing, once considered directed to an objective order, was transformed into a far more subjective epistemology.

Philosophers see "the turn toward the subject" as beginning with Descartes (1596–1650) in the seventeenth century. His successors continued to move from a traditional, receptive epistemology to one that was more constructive. Human knowing was no longer understood as determined by the world it apprehended. Instead, modernity emphasized what the human subject contributes to the process of knowing, a view particularly evident in the philosophy of Immanuel Kant (1724–1804). The human person thus became the measure of all things, with an epistemology that put the emphasis on the subjective, on what the knowing subject contributes.

The sensibility known as postmodernism, a latter-day product of modernity, furthered this process, leading to skepticism about the existence of objective truth. The process of undermining modernity's supreme confidence in an autonomous human reason, unfettered by ecclesial or biblical authorities, was slow but relentless. Nineteenth and early twentieth century thinkers like Kierkegaard, Nietzsche, Marx, and Freud, often called the "masters of suspicion," argued that human knowing was based not on reason alone but shaped by unconscious dynamisms or external conditions. No longer was the human person simply a "rational animal," as philosophers once had claimed.

Søren Kierkegaard (1813–55) stressed the absolute solitude of the person before God who, like Abraham, had to set forth into the unknown. Friedrich Nietzsche (1844–1900) argued that it was not reason but the will to power that dominated our knowing. He saw modern culture as making God irrelevant. The only values are those created by the "superman" who lived beyond good and evil. Karl Marx (1818–33) adopted Hegel's dialectic but secularized it; culture was governed not by Hegel's Absolute but by social realities and economic relationships. Philosophy's task was not to interpret the world, but to change it. Sigmund Freud (1856–1939), in his psychology, portrayed the human person as driven not by reason but by subconscious dynamisms, the id, the superego, and the pleasure principle, beneath which lurked the death wish. Common to these thinkers was the conviction that the human person was not a self-possessed rational being but rather in a state of alienation, another Hegelian concept, driven by unconscious impulses and sinister dynamisms.

The violence and wars of the twentieth century further shattered modernity's confidence that society, governed by reason alone, would continue progressing toward the perfection of humanity. The century saw millions of deaths in two world wars; the horrific bombing of cities, including the use of nuclear weapons; and an increasing chasm between the very affluent and the very poor. It was also a century of dictatorial governments, state-sponsored torture, religiously motivated terrorism, and numerous genocides—from the slaughter of the Armenians during the First World War to today's government-sponsored starvation, violence, and death in the Darfur region of western Sudan that has claimed more than four hundred thousand lives and displaced some 2.5 million people. Today, there are new wars, in Ukraine, and in the Middle East—all evidence of the violence that lurks in the human heart.

The sensibility called postmodernism is a response to this loss of confidence in objective reason and any conviction of unlimited progress. Postmodernism stresses that all knowledge is "socially constructed" based on one's social location, meaning that human perception is filtered and conditioned by issues of race, ethnicity, gender, sexual orientation, and economic status. French poststructuralists provided the philosophical foundation for this view; they posited that all cultural phenomena are primarily linguistic. For

TO BELIEVE OR NOT BELIEVE

Jacques Derrida, all phenomena are "texts," outside of which reality itself remains unknowable. Michel Foucault maintained that all knowledge is an expression of power relationships exercised through social institutions. This being so, postmodernism's characteristic method is deconstruction: tearing down hierarchies, rules, established meanings, and traditional "metanarratives" built on the hegemony of privileged values and power relationships.

Postmodernism's influence has not been entirely negative. It has restored a certain humility to Western thought and made us more aware of the importance of personal circumstances in influencing how we think. In deconstructing the idea of constant progress, it has made us more aware of the problem of evil. Pope Benedict XVI stressed this in his beautiful encyclical *Spe Salvi* ("Saved in Hope"). Thus, a postmodern perspective shows us the tentative character of our knowledge and the limited nature of our perspectives. In doing this, it has uncovered liberating alternatives for oppressed minority groups.

At the same time, the skepticism it has introduced too often has led to a pervasive relativism and suspicion of all truth claims; if all knowledge is based on power relationships, a new culture of victimization, real or imagined, easily develops. Few speak of "truth" today, only "truths," multiple and diverse. If all truths are relative, our "knowledge" itself becomes suspect and objective truth unobtainable. In the words of Ralph Keyes, "Postmodern attitudes toward 'truth' have leaped the walls of the academy and become a key source of our eroding commitment to truth-telling."[2] The very concept of truth is at risk.

In a homily given at the congregation just before he was elected to the papacy, Cardinal Joseph Ratzinger spoke of a "dictatorship of relativism…that does not recognize anything as definitive and whose ultimate goal consists solely of one's own ego and desires."[3] Perhaps his language was a little strong, but others have made similar points. Earlier, we noted Pope Francis's concern about social media spreading fake news and false information, fomenting prejudice and hate.

Poisoned Politics

As Keyes argued, "Deception has become commonplace at all levels of contemporary life."[4] In his book, he shows how right and wrong, including truth telling, were important concepts in the early days of self-help psychology, but when psychotherapy became a kind of secular religion, truth telling became optional, just a symptom of various emotional disorders. In our legal system, a lie not told under oath did not count as such. He uses the example of President Bill Clinton who once observed that the conflicting testimonies of Anita Hill and Supreme Court candidate Clarence Thomas might be seen by a lawyer as an "alternative version of reality."[5] Sounds like Kellyanne Conway's efforts at a press conference to defend President Trump by speaking of "alternative facts." A fact is a given, something real. In the world of higher education, Keyes gives further examples of dishonesty, this time from professors manipulating data in their research, taking credit for the work of their research assistants, or inflating their resumes. Some have claimed falsely to be Vietnam veterans. Faculty colleagues and administrators are often hesitant to respond to revelations of these misdeeds.[6]

Then there is politics. Richard Nixon lied continually about any responsibility for Watergate. Ronald Reagan denied trading arms for hostages in Iran. Bill Clinton lied about his relationship with a young intern. George W. Bush's administration falsely claimed the presence of "weapons of mass destruction" in Iraq to justify the 2003 invasion. Joseph Biden made several false statements about his academic record during an early aborted run for the presidency. These are only a few examples.[7] Today, the problem of post-truth or "fake news," with social media functioning as a force multiplier, is many times worse; it is completely out of control.

TO BELIEVE OR NOT BELIEVE

Contemporary social media platforms, ideologically driven networks like Fox News and Newsmax, and countless blogs have been used to spread false information, prejudice, and conspiracy theories like QAnon as politicians lie for political advantage, poisoning the political process. Fox News settled a $1.6 billion lawsuit brought by Dominion Voting Systems for falsely claiming that their machines had contributed to Trump's loss in 2020. After network owner Rupert Murdoch admitted that they were knowingly endorsing false allegations, the network settled for 787 million dollars. Fox was afraid of losing viewers to the even more conservative Newsmax network.

Under Donald Trump, a post-truth society reached a new high. In an article by Tony Schwartz, Trump's ghostwriter for his 1987 memoir, *The Art of the Deal*, published shortly before his election as president, Schwartz said "Lying is second nature to him....More than anyone else I have ever met, Trump has the ability to convince himself that whatever he is saying at any given moment is true, or sort of true, or at least *ought* to be true."[8] Countless articles describe Trump as a pathological liar. He lied about the size of the crowd at his inauguration on January 20, 2017, and about the election being stolen after President Biden's victory in 2020; thus from the beginning of his presidency to its end, and countless times in between.

According to a March 4, 2020, article in *Boston College Magazine*, "The president of the United States told seventy-three lies. The day before that, he lied forty times. As of April 3, through 1,170 days in office, Donald Trump had made a total of 18,000 demonstrably false or misleading claims. All of this is according to *The Washington Post* Fact Checker, one of several outlets dedicated to analyzing and correcting the exaggerations, misstatements, and flat-out falsehoods of our politicians."[9]

Mark Edmundson describes Trump as a reckless pragmatist, a man who uses words not to express truth or values but to influence his listeners and get what he wants. His followers also "are in on the pragmatic secret that Truth has gone on vacation."[10] In the

2022 midterm election, over two hundred Republican candidates ran on Trump's "Big Lie" that the 2020 election was stolen, against all the evidence, including that of Trump's own Attorney General. Evidence supporting a lack of respect for the truth and civility on the part of some "Trumpers" and other elected representatives is widespread. Republican Mike Johnson, who was elected Speaker of the House in October 2023, after three other candidates failed to gain a majority, played a major role in contesting the 2020 election. Other examples follow.

Marjorie Taylor Greene, a congresswoman from Georgia, has promoted various anti-Semitic, white supremacist, and other conspiracy theories from QAnon and other far right sources. George Santos, a former congressman from New York, falsely fabricated much of his biography, making false claims about his family, education, financial status, property ownership, and charitable works. Lauren Boebert, a congresswoman from Colorado, continued to allege that the 2020 election was stolen and claimed without evidence that hundreds of thousands of Arizona ballots were illegally mailed to voters. She dismissed the congregational investigation of the January 6, 2022, Capitol invasion as a "sham witch hunt," embracing QAnon conspiracy theories. In Florida, Governor Ron DeSantis's administration is trying to control—or better, whitewash—the country's history by banning books on its cultural and institutional racism or by forbidding teachers in public schools from teaching it, but Kamala Harris's unnuanced, occasionally virulent language about abortion rights has not contributed to a more civil dialogue on this issue that has so divided the country. Nor have Nancy Pelosi's comments that restricting abortion rights was a sinful assault on women of color. She has also misrepresented the position of the Catholic Church on abortion.

As falsehoods proliferate and politicians use false narratives, conspiracy theories, and personal attacks to demonize their opponents, truth itself becomes a casualty and the political process is poisoned.

Compromise becomes impossible, paralyzing the process of government.

This is not a problem simply in the United States. Strongmen like Donald Trump, Vladimir Putin, Xi Jinping, Narendra Modi, Viktor Orbán, Nayib Bukele, Daniel Ortega, and Jair Bolsonaro are only the latest who work to control the news.

Moisés Naím calls them the "3P autocrats"—those who employ populism, polarization, and post-truth to hold on to power. Political differences are reduced to absolutist struggles against good and evil. Instead of seeking consensus on difficult issues, they use media celebrity to gain power, collapsing politics into entertainment and party identification into a tribal fan base, always willing to ignore their megastar's transgressions. Others have weaponized political rhetoric in the service of nationalistic populism that further polarizes their societies. Spreading falsehoods, conspiracy theories, personal attacks, distrust of experts, and controlling print and digital media sources, they plant disinformation and confusion in their communities to camouflage their intentions. Truth can be a threat to those in power. In some countries, journalists' lives are at stake. Turkey under Erdoğan has the world's largest number of jailed journalists.[11] In Mexico, at least eighty-six journalists and other media workers have been killed since 2012.

An Increasing Illiteracy

If deliberate falsehoods have poisoned our political process, the increasing reliance of so many on social media for information is contributing to a post-truth society, and even to an increasing illiteracy of sectors of the population. Twitter, Facebook, Instagram, and blogs are no substitute for credible news sources, newspapers, mainstream news programs, scholarly magazines, and journals. Complicated social or political issues cannot be reduced to a Facebook post, a YouTube or TikTok video, a sound bite, or a commentary on Fox News or Newsmax. Jesuit Father General Adolfo Nicolás once spoke of electronic media as contributing to a "globalization of superficiality," a particular challenge to higher education.[12] Worse still, these new technologies use algorithms to give the disaffected and the unbalanced access to millions with similar views, leading easily to violence.

Still, too many Americans today rely on these sources for their information. Some groups are particularly susceptible to these bogus sources, especially those disadvantaged by an increasing economic inequality.

A study from the Public Religion Research Institute (PRRI) says that most white evangelical Protestants (54 percent) claim that the 2020 election was stolen from Trump versus 32 percent for white Catholics and 10 percent for the religiously unaffiliated. Republicans are the most likely to be QAnon believers (27 percent), compared with 19 percent of independents and 8 percent of Democrats. A Pew Research Center study says that 81 percent of white evangelicals voted for Trump in 2016 and even more—84 percent—voted for him in 2020.[13] On voting rights, 85 percent of Republicans say that ineligible voters casting ballots is a bigger problem than denying eligible citizens the right to vote; 83 percent of Democrats say the opposite.[14] White evangelical support for gun rights surpasses that of any other religious group.[15]

Many evangelical Republicans support efforts to declare the United States a Christian nation, based on a false understanding of the founding fathers' intention. "Seventy-eight percent of this group support this, compared to 48 percent of other Republicans."[16] It ignores the fact that the most influential of the founding fathers were Unitarians or Deists. Some Southern states resist any efforts to teach our country's sad history of racial prejudice and violence under the guise of protecting students from Critical Race Theory. History just isn't important. As Robert P. Jones notes, social scientists call this blending of white identity politics with Christianity "white Christian nationalism...the worldview behind Trumpism and the 'Make

America Great Again' movement."[17] White Christian nationalism remains a serious threat to our democracy.

Disinformation

Pope Francis has several paragraphs critical of social media in his encyclical *Fratelli Tutti* (2020). Calling attention to a "frenzy of texting," he points to the emergence of a new lifestyle enabling us to access only what we are interested in and to exclude all that we cannot control. The pope argues that many platforms favor encounters between persons who think alike, shielding them from debate. "These closed circuits facilitate the spread of fake news and false information, fomenting prejudice and hate" (no. 45).

Nor are people better informed when so much of their information comes from social media. Political operatives and foreign agents use artificial intelligence and voice-cloning tools to construct life-like videos of their political opponents appearing to say things that collapse the boundaries between fact and fiction, distributing them to millions on social media.[18] Some may stem from Russian agents, who have already interfered in the American political process. According to an article in the *Wall Street Journal*, the Kremlin's efforts to help elect Donald Trump are a revival of Soviet covert behavior that dates to the Cold War.[19] After the 2016 presidential elections, a federal grand jury in the District of Columbia returned an indictment against twelve Russian military intelligence officers for their alleged roles in interfering with the election. Charges included hacking, identity and document theft, and false registration of a domain.[20] Philip Howard, head of the Oxford Internet Institute, said on CBC News that "92 per cent of the misinformation from state-backed agencies around the world originates from Russia and China."[21]

Digital platforms, often addictive, can create a sense of isolation, leading to a gradual loss of contact with concrete reality. Virtual relations can easily take the place of real ones, leaving people isolated and angry. Algorithms monitor peoples' choices and interests, sending attractive content to keep them connected, not opening them to broader perspectives but simply reinforcing their views. Sound bites replace reasoned opinions, conspiracy theories take the place of objective knowledge. Extremist ideas, once confined to tabloid journals, now profusely populate social media platforms. They can easily result in a dangerous mob psychology, particularly when a charismatic leader emerges. Witness the January 6 Capitol invasion.

Thus, social media platforms are often used to encourage hostility, insults, and verbal violence destructive to others, while they give free reign to ideologies that, until recently, would not have been tolerated. These "closed circuits" facilitate the spread of false information, fomenting prejudice and hate and substituting ideology for objective reporting. The polarization that so divides our communities' political lives, even churches today, is growing. Civility is increasingly absent from our public dialogue and our everyday life. Easy access is given to anyone seeking a platform; there is little vetting of expertise, content, or judgments.

Many people, who lack a critical ability to recognize disinformation or political rhetoric, become captive to conspiracy theories spread by sources such as QAnon or right-wing websites, like the man who attacked Nancy Pelosi's husband with a hammer shortly before the midterm elections in 2022. He was found to have bought into Trump's Big Lie, claimed that the 2020 election was fraudulent, and subscribed to the QAnon story that a cabal of Democrat pedophiles were running a child sex-trafficking ring out of a Washington restaurant. Online conspiracy theories or racist websites close minds and poison attitudes, clouding judgments concerning what is real, and making discernment nearly impossible. They have contributed to the rise in hate crimes, anti-Semitism, and attacks on ethnic or racial groups or on members of the LGBTQ community. Others go on to commit acts of violence, abetted by easy access to guns. According to the Center for Disease Control and Prevention, death by guns in the United States in 2020 included 24,292 suicides and 19,384 murders.

Today, disinformation is an international problem. Repressive states carefully control internet access and content for their own citizens but flood competitive states with disinformation under false titles. Their political operatives use botnets to compromise computer systems, steal data, or attack infrastructures. Hackers engage in "spear phishing" to gain access to personal information or steal identities. Many platforms are not carefully monitored for false narratives, conspiracy theories posted without comment, and personal attacks. The very concept of "facts" has been deconstructed.

Modernity's Skepticism

Dishonesty at every level of contemporary life is not the only factor that weakens our grasp of the real. Modernity's focus on the subject has also contributed to a loss of truth and limited our knowledge to an empirical model. What has been lost is a sense for the transcendent meaning that has characterized Western civilization since its earliest days.

The pre-Socratic philosophers sought to understand the cosmos, not as the work of mythological deities but in terms of rational principles. Their successors were to develop metaphysics, a discipline that sought the underlying ontological principles of reality: being, substance, identity, change, and knowledge. For Plato, the real was not the observable, the world of appearance and change, but the intelligible. He posited a perfect first principle or "God," the source of the ideas or archetypes.

Aristotle brought Plato's ideas down to earth. He sought to explain "being" in terms of ultimate principles: substance, form, matter, the universals, and causality, all set in motion by a divine principle or God that he called the prime or unmoved mover. He denied Plato's idea of a separate world of forms or ideas by holding that universals are incorporeal; they became actual only when instantiated in real things that have a common nature. Universals are known by the active intellect (*intellectus agens*), or in more contemporary terms, by intelligence recognizing the intelligibility in the data. The god of Plato or of Aristotle was a philosophical principle, not a personal deity, and Aristotle was the first to use the term "metaphysics."

Christian theologians were to build on the work of these seminal thinkers; to their metaphysics they added the idea of a personal God who creates out of nothing (*creatio ex nihilo*), developing epistemologies, cosmologies, anthropologies, and systems of ethics, but what was common was the conviction that knowledge comes from contact with the real. While not simply "taking a look," critical intelligence could reach beyond the merely material world of the senses to intuit the transcendent.

With the scientific revolution of the sixteenth century, a new understanding of critical intelligence developed; science insisted on demonstrable or "scientific" knowledge. The Enlightenment, beginning in the eighteenth century, privileged an autonomous reason over more traditional religious, social, and political sources of knowledge. Both the scientific revolution and the Enlightenment tended to introduce a skepticism of any transcendental knowledge, what Roger Haight calls "metaphysical skepticism, relativism, and ontic pessimism."[22] Without freedom, spirit, or purpose, the universe became the product of mere chance, or for some, a mechanism. Ultimate reality remained beyond the reach of intelligence. A modern form of this impoverished theory of knowing is called "scientism," the idea that what cannot be demonstrated is not real. It also leads to a relativism that by placing human beings at the center closes off any openness to transcendence.[23]

The adoption of the scientific method was to lead to great mechanical and technological progress, but its reductionist epistemology, rejecting other ways of knowing, was to contribute to an increasing secularism. The world was stripped of mystery, enchantment, and the transcendent, as Charles Taylor argues in his massive work *A Secular Age*.[24] Belief in human dignity, natural law, let alone God, was seen as alienation of the human spirit or psychological projection. Darwin's theory of evolution led to an even deeper skepticism; conservative Christians saw it as an attack on biblical revelation, thus on any belief in a creator God. For many, it resulted in the false view that science and religion were incompatible, a subject we will consider in a subsequent chapter.

More recently, the so-called new atheists have sold books with provocative titles such as *God Is Not Great: How Religion Poisons Everything* (the late Christopher Hitchens), *The End of Faith: Religion, Terror, and the Future of Reason* (Sam Harris), and *The God Delusion* (Richard Dawkins), which appear to some as the latest deconstruction of any kind of religious knowledge. Their books sold well, but as serious critiques they lack real depth. Richard Dawkins's claim that the notion of God should be subjected to empirical verification like any other hypothesis, as though God were just another object in the world, represents a naïve scientism. Sam Harris naively asks why the Bible, supposedly written by the creator of the universe, has no mathematical insight or information about DNA. Really!

There are serious objections to the existence of God, but they are not to be found here. John Haught, who has some wonderful books on God and evolution, argues that the "engagement with theology on the part of these 'new atheists' lies at about the same level of reflection on faith that one can find in contemporary creationist and fundamentalist literature."[25] Much more serious is the argument from suffering and injustice that we will consider later.

Many philosophies and theologies reject the narrow limitation of knowledge to what can be empirically established. Augustine, shaped by the Neoplatonic tradition he inherited, saw human intelligence drawn by a natural desire for truth and beauty, turning inward or "ascending" from the sensible to the intelligible, from knowledge of objects to knowledge of the self, finally to an awareness of a supreme being that is God or Truth, closer to us than we are to ourselves.

Thomas Aquinas offered his "five ways," not so much proofs as arguments for the existence of God. They can be convincing for those who accept the premises, but they are not demonstrative. The most compelling is his third argument from contingency, based on a recognition that nothing can explain its own existence. He reasoned that all things in nature are generated and corrupted. They are able to be and not to be, but it is impossible for these things always to be, for what is possible not to be sometimes is not. Thus, he concludes to something whose existence is not contingent but necessary, something that does not receive being but gives it to others. This is what we call God, not another being, but pure *Being* itself. In God, existence and essence are the same. God's essence is simply to be. God is not a noun, but a verb, pure actuality.

Aquinas played a major role in bringing Aristotle's thought into the Dominican tradition; Aquinas's approach is intellectual, based on reasoning. Augustine's thought is Platonic. As Joseph Ratzinger/Pope Benedict XVI frequently pointed out, natural reason alone is not enough to see God. The will has a role to play in knowing; one must love truth and the good if one is to know them. Or as Pope Benedict states in his book *Jesus of Nazareth*, the organ for seeing God is the heart.[26]

Very different from secular rationality, Karl Rahner's theological anthropology describes the human person as spirit in the world, open to the absolute. His emphasis is on experience. Indeed, he sees the absolute disclosed against the transcendental horizon of human consciousness. Human knowing or intelligence is constantly reaching behind the finite and what it knows to question what lies beyond. The experience of questioning reveals the transcendental reach of consciousness, an infinite reach to what Rahner describes as a "preapprehension" (*Vorgriff*) of "being as such." While such transcendental knowing is mediated by our knowing concrete realities—the persons or things in the world—it is at the same time a transcendental experience of our orientation toward absolute mystery, which he calls a fundamental experience of God, an awareness that is non-conceptual and unthematic, becoming conceptual and thematic only on reflection.[27]

So, we come to grasp the existence of God, not just by reasoning beyond the world of experience as in Aquinas's five ways, but also by discovering our orientation toward absolute being, goodness, truth, and beauty disclosed in the very structure of our consciousness, but this vision of the human is foreign to most people today, at least in the United States. Our higher education has become increasingly specialized, designed for getting a job.

The Scholastics of the Middle Ages sought to systematize all knowledge. Graduate students at the University of Paris, the premiere center of higher learning at the time, were expected to write their own commentaries on Peter Lombard's *Sentences*, a summary of all the great Christian themes. Catholic colleges and universities, especially those in the Jesuit network, generally had a broadly based core curriculum integrating faith and reason.[28] Along with science, literature, language, and history, students studied philosophy and theology. Today, however, much of that has changed.

Loss of the Humanities

In the United States, education was traditionally based on moral formation. According to David Brooks, however, a shift took place after the Second World War. The traditional view of an objective moral order, developed in community, was abandoned. Instead, the intrinsic goodness of each person was stressed. A moral compass was discovered by getting in touch with one's inner voice. Morality was privatized, but, as Brooks argues, "expecting people to build a satisfying moral and spiritual life on their own by looking within themselves is asking too much. A culture that leaves people morally naked and alone leaves them without the skills to be decent to one another."[29]

With today's emphasis on practical courses in business and STEM-oriented disciplines, many institutions are reducing programs in the liberal arts. "During the past decade, the study of English and history at the collegiate level has fallen by a full third. Humanities enrollment in the United States has declined overall by seventeen percent."[30] Philosophy and theology departments are being downsized.[31] The result is students graduating with an ignorance of theology, history, and the humanities and increasingly narrow specializations. Some use AI to generate their essays and term papers. What is at risk of being lost is any deep humanistic sense of the true, the good, and the beautiful. Instead, they watch TikTok.

Today, the culture of colleges and universities has also changed. Undergraduate students seem increasingly fragile. Rather than confronting new ideas, some of which may be challenging, today's students are overly concerned about their "emotional safety." They want "safe spaces" and administrators to discipline those who commit "microaggressions." New laws require colleges and universities to allow students to bring their emotional support or "comfort animals" to campus. In their article, "The Coddling of the American Mind," Lukianoff and Haidt write about students demanding that administrators protect them from words and ideas they do not like. They ask, "What exactly are students learning when they spend four years or more in a community that polices unintentional slights, places warning labels on works of classic literature, and in many other ways conveys the sense that words can be forms of violence that require strict control by campus authorities, who are expected to act as both protectors and prosecutors?"[32]

Truth

As we conclude this chapter on a post-truth society, we should ask Pilate's question, What is truth? Asking my students this question usually led to interesting answers but few approaching an adequate understanding. The ancient Greeks saw truth as correspondence between the mind of the knower and objects or things in the world. In his *Metaphysics*, Aristotle in describing truth states, "To say of what is that it is not, or of what is not that it is, is false, while to say of what is that it is, and of what is not that it is not, is true." A classic statement of this "correspondence" theory comes from Thomas Aquinas: truth is the adequation or correspondence of the thing and the intellect (*veritas est adaequatio rei et intellectus*). For Aquinas, the intellect reveals the spiritual dimension of the human, constantly reaching beyond the object known toward the absolute, toward God who is absolute Oneness, Truth, Goodness, and Beauty. He describes the "intellectual light" of the human intellect as "nothing more than a participating likeness of the uncreated light."[33]

To know the truth is to see something for what it is, not as what we think or would like it to be, but grasping truth means more than simply taking a look. Truth is different from opinion. A more contemporary theory of truth seeks to distinguish common sense or naïve realism from critical realism. One might conclude that the earth was the center of the universe from watching the sun "rise" and "set," or assume a deterministic universe from the apparent regularity of physical laws, or draw false conclusions from the Scriptures from a literal reading of the text.

Discovering truth sometimes calls on us to change our minds and move in a different direction. Scott Hahn is a noted Catholic biblical scholar and evangelist. Raised Presbyterian, by his own admission he hated the Catholic Church and preached against it, but his study of the Scriptures and theology led him, almost against his will, to see the truth of Catholic teaching and ultimately into the Church, followed later by his wife, Kimberly.[34]

To discover truth, we need to think critically, to move beyond the senses and the conventional. Answering a difficult question, or finding the intelligibility in the data, whether it is a scientific problem, a theological question, a social issue, or a personal relationship, usually requires some investigation into its context or history, whether scientific, theological, cultural, or personal. This is why we have laboratories and libraries or need to examine our consciences. An opinion, sound bite, or social media post is rarely sufficient, yet these are the sources of information for so many today.

If we are not to become a virtually illiterate society, we need a more informed, better educated population. We need to help young people learn how to distinguish the rational or the factual from the merely rhetorical. They need to develop the ability to evaluate information, to question and discern. Catholic higher education once sought to teach these skills. Students took courses in logic and philosophy to develop critical thinking. They were taught, sometimes even in high school, how to recognize logical or rhetorical fallacies, among them, the ad hominem argument, the red herring, the false dilemma, the non sequitur or *post hoc ergo propter hoc*, the hasty generalization, or the straw man, but this kind of education is too often a thing only of the past.

Conclusion

Truth is precious. Our intelligence is ordered toward truth, and toward God. Today, however, we live in what many call a post-truth society. Our social institutions are polarized, our politics poisoned with suspicion, dismissive language, and name calling. Our communities are fractured by mutual hostility. As I have argued, however, the roots of the contemporary loss of truth are deeper than our divisive politics.

Modernity's focus on the subject introduced an epistemological shift from what consciousness receives from the world it knows to what it contributes to the knowing process. The postmodern ethos in a later reaction challenged modernity's confidence in autonomous reason, bringing to light hidden psychological dynamisms and the conditioning of knowing by personal circumstance. In addition to a profound suspicion of metanarratives and truth claims, the tragedies and violence of the twentieth century shattered any belief in continual progress toward a better life and society.

In his 2007 encyclical *Spe Salvi*, Pope Benedict XVI quotes the Frankfurt philosopher and social critic Theodor Adorno, who once said, "Progress, seen accurately, is progress from the sling to the atom bomb" (no. 22). If postmodernity gives a certain humility toward all truth claims, negatively it has often resulted in a profound suspicion toward truth itself in our public discourse. In a post-truth society, politicians and television commentators lie and appeal to conspiracy theories without consequence.

So, what does all this have to do with so many young adults leaving behind their churches and their faith? I have tried to describe the world in which they live, at least in the West. The transcendent reach of intelligence is no longer recognized; metaphysical skepticism predominates. Scientism has replaced other modes of knowing. In the United States especially, truth is no longer honored. Religious truth is disparaged or ignored.

These are not the only causes of disaffiliation; the influence of parents, teachers, and friends remains of primary importance. In today's world, however, the cultural elites too often dismiss faith as fantasy. A sense for the transcendent has been lost and many mistakenly take for granted an irreconcilable conflict between faith and science, as we will see in the next chapter. It is difficult to be a person of faith without personal and cultural support. This is the world our young people inhabit. For them, God has become an unnecessary hypothesis.

To know and to know what is true is to know what is. While not always an easy process, it means discovering meaning, intelligibility, and truth in what we experience. It is to reach out toward the absolute that is implicitly revealed in every act of knowing. In this way, we realize the deepest potential of our nature, that orientation of our intellects and our desires towards the divine.

3
Faith and Reason

ALL TOO OFTEN, I hear from young people that they find it difficult to believe in the Christian story. Struggling with their faith, it all seems incredible in a world where the scientific outlook prevails, and people want hard evidence for what they believe. They find the biblical narratives mythological, not understanding that myths in a prescientific age are ways of teaching some moral or religious truth. So, we should ask: Is there a conflict between faith and reason, between religion and science?

A 2015 Pew Center survey reported that 76 percent of those without any religious affiliation were the most likely to think that science and religion were often in conflict. William Dinges cites two studies that stress a conflict between faith and science as one of the reasons given by a significant number of young Americans for dropping out of their churches.[1]

Yet many young Catholics are unaware of the long-standing Catholic principle that faith and reason are complementary. In this chapter, we will take a deeper look at this principle. First, we will consider theology and science as different ways of knowing, with different understandings of what counts as evidence, the different ways Protestant and Catholic biblical interpretation developed after the Reformation, and the long tradition of learning from secular wisdom. Then, we will look briefly at some of the scientific achievements of Catholic scholars, both lay and clerical, and the development of Catholic theology in modern times, especially after the Second Vatican Council.

Theology and Science

As Pope John Paul wrote in his 1990 apostolic constitution on Catholic colleges and universities, *Ex Corde Ecclesiae*, the modern university was born "from the heart of the church." In the early middle ages, major monasteries established schools to educate young monks who needed to be literate for liturgical prayer, transcribing classical texts, and keeping monastic records. Other schools developed around the great cathedrals, usually sponsored by a religious community. In addition to religious studies, their curricula included the *trivium*, grammar, rhetoric, and logic; and the *quadrivium*, courses in mathematics, music, law, and astronomy; and eventually medicine, law, and theology. As instruction was in Latin, such a school was known as a *universitas magistrorum et scholarium*, a society or community of teachers and scholars, a "university."

With the recovery of the more empirical thought of Aristotle in the twelfth century, the universities turned more attention to the natural sciences, but there was never any thought that theology and science were antithetical to each other. One deals with the observable world of nature, the other with traces of the transcendent and its impact on the human spirit. Both are concerned with discovering truth, which is ultimately one. To posit one truth of religion and another contrary truth of science would be to embrace some illegitimate theory of "alternative truths," in contradiction to each other.

Theology, on the one hand, is critical reflection on faith; St. Anselm (d. 1109) defined theology as *fides quaerens intellectum*, "faith seeking understanding." Faith comes from the religious experience of a people. From a Christian perspective, faith is based ultimately on God's free self-disclosure through prophetic interpretation and the story of Jesus, in other words, on revelation. Usually grounded in sacred texts, theology seeks to corelate a received religious tradition in the context of the lived experience of a people.

On the other hand, science is empirical. It investigates natural phenomena with systematic observation, experimentation, and the development of explanatory hypotheses. It seeks to understand the laws, characteristics, and relationships that govern our existence, both material and social, making hypotheses and trying to verify them. While what may be true theologically is of a different order and cannot be proved scientifically, good theology is frequently interdisciplinary, relying on different scientific disciplines. The two should not be confused.

For example, in talking about God's creative work, theology deals with creation's ultimate cause or source; science may describe cosmic origins, evolutionary development, and the laws governing the natural world, but the question of ultimate causality lies beyond it. It properly answers scientific questions, not those of theology. Biblical fundamentalists frequently ignore scientific explanations in favor of a biblical literalism, while some scientists reduce all knowledge to what is empirically verifiable, what we earlier called scientism. Or as Galileo said long ago, citing Cardinal Baronius (1598), "The Bible was written to show us how to go to heaven, not how the heavens go."

In his 1998 encyclical on faith and reason *Fides et Ratio*, Pope John Paul II stressed the complementarity of the two: "Faith and reason are like two wings on which the human spirit rises to the contemplation of truth; and God has placed in the human heart a desire to know the truth—in a word, to know himself" (no. 1). Similarly, Joseph Ratzinger said, "Reason needs to listen to the great religious traditions if it does not wish to become deaf, blind, and mute concerning the most essential elements of human existence."[2] At the same time, without critical reason, faith too often risks a collapse into fundamentalism.

In a famous dialogue with Jürgen Habermas, a philosopher of the Neo-Marxist Frankfurt School, Ratzinger and Habermas debated whether modern nations could justify the human rights they presupposed without a metaphysical or religious foundation. Answering in the affirmative, Habermas appealed to social consensus. Ratzinger answered that such a foundation was too fragile. The political polarization and lack of mutual respect we see today suggests that Ratzinger was correct.

Interpreting the Bible

Catholicism is far from being a fundamentalist faith. While the sixteenth-century reformers generally honored the church's tradition, their lifting up Scripture as the near exclusive principle of authority for Christian faith soon led to the principle, *sola scriptura*, Scripture alone. Protestant scholars assumed that the meaning of the Bible was clear and could interpret itself, but that assumption began to break down with the Enlightenment, privileging reason over against biblical and church authority. As the presumed "clarity of Scripture" broke down in the decades following the Enlightenment under the influence of critical scholarship, Protestant theology developed in two opposing directions. One stressed a critical approach to Scripture that too often uncritically accepted an Enlightenment rationalism, resulting in a theological liberalism that rejected the supernatural, biblical miracles and eschatology, and in many cases, even the resurrection.

The other approach turned to a biblical literalism in conscious opposition to the "slippery slope" of liberal theology. In 1895, the Biblical Congress at Niagara, New York, adopted the term *fundamentalism* to safeguard what it regarded as the "five points of fundamentalism": the verbal inerrancy of Scripture, the virginal birth of Jesus Christ, the doctrine of substitutionary atonement, the physical resurrection of Christ, and his imminent bodily return to earth.

Faith and Reason

This "literalist" approach to Scripture soon spread to other parts of the world and, in addition to the United States, is still followed even today by conservative Christians in much of Latin America, Africa, and Asia.

The compatibility of faith and reason moves beyond a biblical literalism. The Bible's religious truth is mediated by language, symbol, and story. Faith speaks of God's self-disclosure in the stories and prophetic voices of the Hebrew Scriptures and in the life, death, and resurrection of Jesus. That faith must always be expressed in a theological language that is faithful to Scripture and the tradition, and at the same time in harmony with the truths of scientific and philosophical reason.

While Catholics also reverence the Bible as God's word, celebrate it in their liturgy, expound it in their catechetics, and make it central to their theology and pastoral life, they recognize that, although inspired, Scripture always needs to be interpreted. Catholic interpretation is critical, however, not fundamentalist; what is important is not the exact meaning of the words but what the writer intended to communicate. In his important 1943 encyclical, *Divino Afflante Spiritu*, Pope Pius XII opened critical biblical methodology using historical and literary disciplines to Catholic scholars, provided that it didn't conflict with faith and morals. This was to revolutionize the Catholic approach to Scripture. The Second Vatican Council and subsequent decisions of the Pontifical Biblical Commission furthered this development.

As the Council taught in its Dogmatic Constitution on Divine Revelation (*Dei Verbum*), "Since God speaks in Sacred Scripture through men in human fashion, the interpreter of Sacred Scripture, in order to see clearly what God wanted to communicate to us, should carefully investigate what meaning the sacred writers really intended, and what God wanted to manifest by means of their words" (DV 12). In 1993, the Vatican's Pontifical Biblical Commission (PBC) published an important instruction titled "The Interpretation of the

Bible in the Church." The document specifically rejects fundamentalist interpretations of Scripture.

The PBC text points out that fundamentalist literalism is right to insist on the divine inspiration of Scripture, the inerrancy of the word of God (though this must be correctly understood), and the biblical truths contained in the five fundamentals, but it argues that fundamentalism approaches the biblical text as though it were dictated word for word by God, an Islamic rather than a Christian approach. Rooted in an ideology that rejects asking questions or employing critical research methods, it refuses to consider the historical development of revelation, and it fails to recognize that the biblical authors were limited in their capacities and resources or that they made use of different literary forms.

One thinks of the famous 1925 trial in Tennessee in which public high school teacher John Scopes was prosecuted for teaching evolution, a battle that continues today in some conservative states. Even today, most evangelical Christians follow a literalist or "inerrantist" approach to the biblical text, holding that it is true, without error, in all its affirmations, whether in history, science, or literary origins. In short, for the fundamentalist the meaning of the text is identified by what the words say, not by what the writer might have intended to teach. It is a position dictated by traditional beliefs, not critical reason.

The Catholic approach to Scripture is very different. Catholic scholars seek the *literal sense* of the text, not what the words say literally as, for example, in the story of Noah and the flood, but the precise meaning intended by the author. To do this, the biblical scholar uses various literary and historical disciplines to uncover the historical background at the time the text was written. Form criticism identifies the various types or species of literature in a passage, whether poetry, myth, patriarchal legend, prophetic oracle, or law codes, or in the New Testament, sayings of Jesus, parables, miracle stories, liturgical formulae, or apocalyptic sayings, just to name a few. Redaction criticism, sometimes called literary criticism, seeks to find the specific concerns of an author and his literary style. Source criticism tries to find the sources behind an author's work; for example, Matthew and Luke's Gospels are dependent on Mark's, but also have access to the "Q source," a collection of the sayings of Jesus that do not appear in Mark. Both have material unique to their own Gospels. Textual criticism seeks to establish the critical or original text, which may have been expanded by later copyists.

In the case of the story of the flood in Genesis 6 and 7, the point of the story is not God's regret for his creative work because of human sinfulness, and decision to "wipe out from the earth the men whom I have created," along with all the beasts and animals, but rather the destruction that sin has brought into the world, readmitting the chaos that God originally overcame in creating the heavens and the earth. It teaches us that human sinfulness is damaging, not just to human beings, but to creation itself, which is certainly true. To teach this important lesson, the biblical author made use of the *Epic of Gilgamesh*, an ancient Mesopotamian epic poem that predates the Genesis story by at least 1,500 years. It contains a Mesopotamian story of the great flood, filled with monsters and gods, gods who themselves are terrified by the flood.

In addition to the historical critical method, Catholic biblical scholarship has long used other "hermeneutics" or interpretative methods. The *Spiritual Sense* seeks to identify how a particular text might support Christian life and discipleship, for example, rooting it in the Paschal Mystery or the life of Christ. A *Typological Interpretation*, popular in the early church, would see in a biblical narrative a foreshadowing of some person or moment in the life of the church, for example, the flood as a symbol of baptism, or the manna in the desert, "Bread from Heaven," as a foreshadowing of the Eucharist. Melito of Sardis, a late second-century bishop, used images from Isaiah as types to describe Christ's resurrection: "*He was led like a sheep to the slaughter*, yet he was not a sheep. He was silent as a lamb, yet he was not a lamb. The type has passed away; the reality has come."

TO BELIEVE OR NOT BELIEVE

The *Fuller Sense* sees a meaning that goes beyond the literal sense of the text but is to be considered divinely inspired. For example, Isaiah 7:14 says in the Hebrew version, "The virgin [*almah*] shall be with child." *Almah* means literally a "young, unmarried woman," not technically a virgin. The Greek Septuagint translation uses *parthenos*, virgin, which is the way the Isaiah text is usually translated, reflecting the church's belief in the virginity of Mary.

While the literal sense of Scripture is the most important, the other approaches have long been traditional for church life and theology, but what is most important is to interpret a biblical text within the living tradition of the church itself. The church does this especially in its liturgy. It does violence to a text to reduce it to mere history, to "demythologize" it according to rationalist principles, or to see it as merely cultural. Too much of contemporary exegesis falls into this trap. Sandra Schneiders critiques this approach, charging that "for critical biblical scholars the Bible came to be for all practical purposes an exclusively historical document rather than a revelatory or spiritually fruitful one."[3]

What the PBC document calls "actualizing" a text means reading it within the life of the church: "Already within the Bible itself…one can point to instances of actualization: very early texts have been reread in the light of new circumstances and applied to the contemporary situation of the people of God. The same basic conviction necessarily stimulates believing communities of today to continue the process of actualization." This process takes place especially when the text is read within the life and liturgy of the church, allowing it to be revelatory when interpreted and deepened in light of the church's living tradition.

Learning from Secular Wisdom

This critical approach to the church's sacred texts and its faith is not something new in Christian history. Since the earliest days of the church, Christians have been concerned to enter a dialogue with culture. It is usually willing to learn from secular culture. In the Catholic tradition, this is expressed in the principle that sees faith and reason as compatible.

It is only honest to point out that there have been embarrassing moments in Catholicism's history when that principle has not been respected. For example, in a classic case of papal overreach, Pope Boniface VIII in his bull *Unam Sanctam* (1302) claimed "that it is absolutely necessary for the salvation of all men that they submit to the Roman Pontiff" (DS 875), but this teaching was not received by the church. In 1633, Galileo Galilei, after years of controversy with the Inquisition over the theory of heliocentrism, was sentenced to house arrest for the rest of his life. Galileo was right, of course, but controversy remains to this day over the exact nature of his offense. He was not charged with heresy.

Darwin's theory of evolution was another challenge, only gradually accepted by the Church. In his 1950 encyclical, *Humani Generis*, Pope Pius XII taught that Catholics could believe in evolution, but only if they recognized that "souls are immediately created by God" (no. 36). Many Catholics today would recognize God's agency throughout the evolutionary process, without need for a special intervention. Pope Pius also insisted that Catholic faith did not permit accepting a polygenetic origin of humankind, as it was not compatible with the belief in original sin, stemming from an actual sin committed by the first man, Adam, and passed on to his descendants, but the origin of humanity from a single or multiple set of parents is a scientific question, not a theological one.

Pope John Paul II was more confident about evolutionary theory. In a 1996 message to the Pontifical Academy of Scientists, he wrote that that "some new findings lead us toward the recognition of evolution as more than a hypothesis."[4] Still, in echoing Pope Pius's concerns, he stressed that human beings, created in the image and likeness of God for union with himself are of a different ontological order and therefore can never be reduced to a means to some end. That also is Catholic teaching.

As a final example, we might consider Vatican II moving beyond the propositional model of revelation so long presumed by both Protestants and Catholics, an approach that tends to reduce God's mysterious self-communication to verbal formulas or doctrinal statements. God does not reveal himself in theological categories; he does not give theological lectures. Avery Dulles gives numerous examples of such propositional understandings of revelation on the part of both evangelicals and Catholics. For example, Francis Schaeffer wrote that "God has spoken in a linguistic propositional form, truth concerning himself and truth concerning man, history, and the universe."[5] Or for a Catholic example, Dulles quotes a Catholic theologian who asserted that "all declarations (*sententiae*) of Scripture are infallibly true."[6] The Council of Trent came close to such an understanding of revelation when it spoke of the Gospel as the "truth and rules...contained in the written books and unwritten traditions which have come down to us, having been received by the apostles from the mouth of Christ himself" (DS 1501).

In contrast, *Dei Verbum* taught that the deepest truth about God is to be found in Christ himself who is both the mediator and the fullness of all revelation (DV 2). Yet Jesus did not give theological lectures; he told stories and used aphorisms. In the Council's view, revelation is primarily personal and christological, not propositional; it is not to be found in a text or a formula but in the life, teaching, death, and resurrection of Jesus. While these above examples show an appeal to exaggerated understanding of Church authority, or a reluctance to admit new evidence, or a need for further theological reflection, they also illustrate the Church's ability to correct missteps as its tradition continues to develop. Knowledge of history is important. The tradition is living, not set in stone.

Despite these embarrassing moments, the Catholic tradition has always sought to learn from secular wisdom and to deepen and transform it with respect to the Gospel. Perhaps the earliest example of this can be found as Christianity began moving out from its origins in the Hebrew Scriptures and New Testament and into the culture of the Greco-Roman world. The language of Scripture is often mythopoeic, recognizing that "myth" does not necessarily mean something that is false, but the way of explaining in a prescientific age some religious truth or natural event. The authors of the books of the Old Testament did this, using popular myths, stories, tribal and literary narratives, reshaped by prophetic interpretations. So too, the authors of the New Testament, most of them Jews, adopted the messianic, apocalyptic, and wisdom traditions of the Hebrew Scriptures, and drew on them.

Because the message of the Gospel was universal, addressed to all people, it was important to find an appropriate language in which to express it, but the culture of the Greco-Roman world was quite different from that of the biblical authors. Influenced by the Pre-Socratic philosophers and by seminal thinkers like Plato and Aristotle, it sought to explain the world of experience, not in the imaginative language of the Scriptures, but in terms of ultimate causes and a philosophical vocabulary. Its language was more abstract and philosophical, an ontological or metaphysical language as we saw earlier. In many ways it represented the intellectual or scientific language of the day—helpful for expressing the Christian mystery within the dominant Roman Empire but also posing certain challenges. It could be used to express the faith of the church in its emerging doctrinal tradition, although with care not simply to "Hellenize" the faith.

The early church fathers came from this culture. While some were cautious about engaging with a philosophical wisdom considered "pagan," others like Justin Martyr (d. 165) and Clement of Alexandria (d. ca. 215) drew on elements of Greco-Roman philosophy to express their faith. Justin, born to a Greek family in what today is Nabulus in the West Bank, studied Stoicism and Pythagorean thought before becoming a Platonist. Discovering Christianity and embracing it, he saw it as the true philosophy, and incorporated elements of these non-Christian sources to express it. He found in these systems the "seeds of Christianity," concepts such as the impassibility of God, the Logos, and the immortality of the soul, before eventually moving to Rome where he established a school.

Clement, whose official name was Titus Flavius Clemens, was educated in Greek philosophy and literature. A convert also, he drew on Greek philosophy in his theology, although—because some of his writings were controversial—the Greek Church ceased his veneration in the tenth century, while the Latin Church withdrew his name from the Roman Martyrology in 1586. Among Clement's students was Origen, another Christian thinker who drew on Platonic thought in constructing his theology. An exception to this "dialogue" with culture was Tertullian (d. 220) who famously asked, "What has Athens to do with Jerusalem?"

The Hellenistic philosophy used by some of the church fathers was not without some danger, for the church's faith and its impact can still be felt today. The Greek philosophical tradition was highly dualistic, privileging spirit over matter, the eternal over the temporal, the idea over real things in the world, while the divine was conceived as immutable, free from passion, and utterly transcendent. The Christology of Arius, seeing the Word as an intermediary between the divine and creation, a kind of demigod, was a classic expression of Greek thought for those who found the concept of the incarnation utterly foreign.

So, there was a need for caution. Still, the fathers were not involved in speculation; their concern was always finding the language to express the church's faith in a way appropriate to the culture of the day. Their concern was evangelical. The two great fourth-century catechetical schools—one at Alexandria in Egypt, the other at Antioch in Syria—used contemporary philosophical language, concepts such as substance, nature, person, the "same being" (*homoosious*, consubstantial) as opposed to "in like being," to safeguard the church's christological faith in language that was intelligible to their contemporaries and still faithful to the biblical witness.

Their efforts were to bear fruit in the christological confession of faith or creed of the Council of Chalcedon (451).

The theology of St. Augustine (d. 430), perhaps one of the most influential theologians in Western Christian history, was profoundly shaped by the Platonic and Neoplatonic philosophy he discovered in his youthful search for truth. His thought has continued to shape Western theology. Joseph Ratzinger/Pope Benedict XVI has acknowledged his debt to both Plato and Augustine.

The great thirteenth-century Dominican, Thomas Aquinas, was to move beyond Platonic thought by his adopting the philosophy of Aristotle, just then being rediscovered in the West, as we noted earlier. Largely preserved by Arab scholars, Aristotle's thought came into Europe through Arab Spain and was increasingly taken up by twelfth-century university scholastics, especially by Aquinas, who thus introduced a new, more empirical philosophical framework for theology. His great work, the *Summa Theologiae*, draws on philosophical reasoning as well as faith. His *Summa Contra Gentiles* rejected an approach to theology that relied on faith alone. "They hold a plainly false opinion who say that in regard to the truth of religion it does not matter what a person thinks about creation so long as he has the correct opinion concerning God. An error concerning the creation ends in false thinking about God" (CG, 2.3). He was careful to reject any contradiction between reason and faith.

The Problem of Suffering

Perhaps the most serious objection to the question, does God exist, is the problem of suffering and evil. For all the beauty of this world, the earth with its spacious skies, majestic mountains, and amber waves of grain, or its beautiful globe shining blue and white against the darkness of space, for so many millions our world is a world of suffering, injustice, and tragedy. Hunger is still a daily reality for millions, grinding poverty forces them to live in unhealthy squalor, without adequate education or opportunities. Much of this is due to human willfulness, a self-interest that ignores the common good, or uses dishonest practices, political power, or violence to advance their personal interests. Many people die from disease or pandemics, while wars and terrorism claim the lives of countless innocent men, women, and children. Social inequities are built into societies, while many populations are ruled by strong men with little concern for human rights, equal opportunity, or the vulnerable.

Some disasters are simply from the forces of nature. They erupt, taking millions of lives. They are not caused by God or sent from him as punishment for human sinfulness as some fundamentalist preachers allege. A material world is imperfect, or better, unfinished; its laws are not absolute but encompass a certain indeterminacy. Natural development is sometimes impaired. Cancers develop, atmospheric conditions produce devasting storms, tectonic plates shift, causing massive earthquakes like the one that took over fifty thousand lives in Turkey and Syria in 2023, or are followed by devasting tsunamis or tidal waves, all punishing displays of nature's power.

Still, it is true that so much suffering comes from the evil that continues to lurk in the human heart, but God often gets the blame. Why did God permit the Shoah, where so many perished, victims of a government-sponsored persecution and highly organized extermination program driven by a vicious racism? Why so many genocides? What does one say to the parents of a beloved child killed in a school shooting? So many tragedies, so many broken hearts. So many people cry out with Archibald MacLeish's figure J. B. in his modern retelling of the biblical story of Job, "If God is good He is not God. If God is God He is not good."

While the problem of suffering remains a mystery, part of our tendency to blame God stems from a flawed theology that attributed all that happens to the divine agency, and thus makes God responsible also for evil. Our different ways of imagining the divine results in different theological conceptions or "models," several that have been popularized in the work of Sallie McFague. She suggests the world as God's body, a pantheistic model; another of God as mother, lover, or friend; or the traditional monarchical model.[7] I would like to suggest several, adapting somewhat her work, suggesting some contemporary models operative in the ways people imagine God today.

The Cosmic Architect. Fundamentally a deist model, this model stems from the seventeenth-century scientific revolution that imagined God as a divine architect who creates the universe and established its laws, then leaves it to run accordingly. This represents a scientist's God, a divine clockmaker who gives the world order and design but is not engaged with it personally, a God who remains distant.

The Divine Monarch. This model had its origins in medieval Christian thought that stressed God's omnipotence, and Reformation theology, especially John Calvin's with his emphasis on the divine sovereignty. Behind it is a premodern worldview, based on a fundamentalist reading of the Old Testament; the psalms addressed God as King (Pss 93, 95, 96, 97, 99), ruling over Israel, the nations, and creation itself. This all-powerful God governed creation, intervening, when necessary, sometimes with miracles that were understood as the divine agency suspending the laws of nature, but the world has its own causality. Does God intervene to strike down sinners? Does he will the death of the innocent or take a child from its loving parents? Does he permit evil to accomplish the divine purpose?

Without a meaningful theory of secondary causality, theology fails to deal adequately with human freedom and ends up making God responsible for evil, either directly or indirectly, as a literal reading of the Old Testament could suggest. For example, according to the First Book of Samuel, God ordered King Saul to slaughter the Amalekites, king, men, women, children, infants, and all their animals (1 Sam 15:3) and then removed him from the kingship when he disobeyed.

Fundamentalist preachers often ascribe human tragedy and natural disasters to God's wrath. Television evangelist Pat Robertson claimed that the 2010 earthquake that killed half a million Haitians was sent by God for their "pact with the devil" to drive out the French in the Haitian revolution (1791–1804), and that the September 11 attacks and Hurricane Katrina were divine punishments for our sins, but this way of thinking makes God a tyrannical monarch, not a compassionate Father. As the poet Annie Dillard says so well, "God is no more blinding people with glaucoma, or testing them with diabetes, or purifying them with spinal pain, or choreographing the seeding of tumor cells through lymph, or fiddling with chromosomes, than he is jimmying floodwaters or pitching tornados at towns."[8]

Moralistic Therapeutic Deism. We saw earlier the cultural image of God that Christian Smith and Melinda Lundquist Denton profile from their research on teenagers; a God who creates and orders the world, wants people to be nice and happy, but does not need to be involved in their lives. They find that "religious languages and vocabularies of commitment, duty, faithfulness obedience, calling, obligation, accountability, and ties to the past are nearly absent" from their discourse.[9]

And there are other ways of imagining the divine. *Pantheism* sees God as present in all things, collapsing any transcendence between God and creation. Karl Barth and some other Protestant theologians proposed a *dialectical God* that restricts God's agency to human subjectivity, an actualist theology that tends to find God's presence only in human subjectivity.

Catholic Scholars and Scientists

Throughout the long history of the Church, Catholic scholars and scientists have made important discoveries in their research. Wikipedia gives two different lists of Catholic scholars, one of lay men and women, the other of clergy. Beyond figures like Nicholas Copernicus and Galileo, I could mention among the most well-known Hildegard of Bingen (d. 1179), a German Benedictine nun, philosopher, medical researcher, and polymath, considered the founder of German natural science; Matteo Ricci (d. 1610), an Italian Jesuit missionary to China, an astronomer and mathematician; he and his convert Xu Guangqi translated Euclid's *Elements* into Chinese; Maria Gaetana Agnesi (d. 1799), a mathematician, studied differential and integral calculus and was the first woman to write a mathematical textbook; André-Marie Ampère (d. 1836) identified the basic unit of electricity; Louis Braille (d. 1852), accidentally blinded as a child, by the age of fifteen had invented most of the code alphabet that bears his name; Louis Pasteur (d. 1857) discovered the process of pasteurization; Gregor Mendel (d. 1884), an Austrian friar, considered the father of genetics; Marie Curie (d. 1934), an astrophysicist who did pioneer work on radioactivity. She was awarded two Nobel prizes. Guglielmo Marconi (d. 1937) is credited with the invention of the radio and the development of wireless telegraphy; and Georges Lemaître (d. 1966), a Belgian priest and theoretical physicist, proposed the "Big Bang" theory on the origin of the universe.

Today, at least thirty-five craters on the moon are named for Jesuits, recognizing their work in the fields of astronomy, mathematics, and physics, and that work continues. My late classmate, William R. Stoeger (d. 2014) was a Jesuit priest, astronomer, and theologian known widely in his field for his research on black holes. He served on the staff of the Vatican Observatory. Recently, an asteroid was named after him. Guy J. Consolmagno, a Jesuit brother and astronomer, is presently director of the Observatory. His research focuses on meteorites and asteroids and other small bodies in the solar system.

I rehearse the names of these scholars as examples of men and women whose faith in no way interfered with their scientific accomplishments. Far from being a fundamentalist faith that sees a conflict between science and religion, Catholicism finds God's presence disclosed within the complexities of the universe, while recognizing that creation has its own laws and dynamics that are open to empirical investigation. From the earliest days of the Church, Christians have sought to learn from wisdom figures, even from those outside the church. To investigate the complexities of creation is to honor the Creator.

Beyond Neo-Scholasticism

Catholic theological investigation is not limited to the biblical witness. For several centuries, its theology was too often confined to an inherited, largely medieval Neo-Scholasticism. Joseph Ratzinger himself says that he found it abstract, dry, and lifeless. For him, the theology of Augustine was more nourishing. In the nineteenth and early twentieth centuries, steps were taken by some scholars and the church itself to enable theology to take advantage of modern historical and biblical studies. John Henry Newman in England as well as Johann Sebastian Drey and Johannes Adam Möhler of the Tübingen School in Germany brought careful historical studies into their theological work. Transcendental Thomism represented an effort on the part of Catholic scholars like Pierre Rousselot and Joseph Maréchal to move beyond the dominant Neo-Scholasticism of the day by entering a dialogue with modern philosophy, especially through the transcendental method of Kant. Transcendental Thomism was to play a significant role in the development of Karl Rahner's theology. Also important was a new emphasis on experience.

Pope Pius XII's encyclical, *Divino Afflante Spiritu* (1943), freed Catholic biblical scholars to use the historical critical disciplines, developed largely by German scholars. The so-called *nouvelle théologie* or new theology describes a movement in France before and after the Second World War that used a historical method called *ressourcement*, a "return to the sources" of Catholic faith in the Scriptures, liturgy, and fathers of the church. Although using this historical approach rather than the dominant Neo-Scholasticism drew down ecclesial sanctions on theologians like Dominicans Yves Congar and Marie-Dominique Chenu, as well as Jesuits Jean Daniélou and Henri de Lubac, their work and that of others was to bear great fruit at the Second Vatican Council.

The Second Vatican Council

An earlier fear of critical scholarship changed with the Second Vatican Council (1962–65), Pope St. John XXIII's efforts to renew the church and update its teachings and life (*aggiornamento*). His famous metaphor for the conciliar process was to open a window, to let in a little fresh air. The Council allowed much of the world to see bishops openly disputing issues on the floor of St. Peter's Basilica, and its sixteen documents—constitutions, declarations, and decrees—did much to renew the church and bring it into the twentieth century.

The monarchical model of church authority and structure was replaced with a collegial model, bringing the bishops into a share in the church's governance and teaching authority, even recognizing their share in the church's infallibility with and under the Bishop of Rome. The Council, for the first time, took steps to develop a theology of the laity, calling all the baptized to a full share in the church's mission. The liturgy was renewed and soon celebrated in the language of the people. An important Pastoral Constitution moved the church from its fortress-church mindset against the world to see it as attentive to "the joys and the hopes, the griefs and the anxieties of the men of this age, especially those who are poor or in any way afflicted" (*Gaudium et Spes*). It encouraged the laity to study theology, previously a clerical discipline, resulting in its laicization, and in the United States, a theological renaissance. The Catholic Church also officially embraced the ecumenical movement, begun almost fifty years earlier by Protestant Christians, and it reached out to dialogue with and learn from other religious traditions, including the Jews, taking steps against the anti-Judaism and anti-Semitism in which the Catholic Church too often had been complicit.

In many ways, the Council set the agenda for the future. When I was a boy, Catholic life and theology were largely untroubled. Seminaries were full of candidates for the priesthood and religious orders had so many vocations that many were building new novitiates and houses of formation. Parishes had numerous priests, and Catholic schools were staffed by large communities of religious women who educated several generations of Catholic children. Theology was still under the tight control of the Holy Office, once called the Office of the Inquisition. Theologians whose works did not pass Vatican scrutiny for orthodoxy had them placed on the Index of Forbidden Books (*Index Librorum Prohibitorum*), and they were disciplined, forbidden to publish or teach. When I first came to my university to teach in 1967, I had to retrieve Teilhard de Chardin's major work, *The Phenomenon of Man*, from "Gehenna," the library's closed storage for books on the Index. Most Catholics were obedient to church teaching; dissent was virtually unknown, or at least not talked about publicly, but all that was to change.

Theological Pluralism

In the postconciliar period, a new emphasis on relating theology to ordinary experience led to the method of correlation that tries to mediate between Scripture and reason as well as between science and faith. For example, in his work, David Tracy tries to correlate theology with contemporary experience. This leads to numerous "contextual" theologies and a theological pluralism, exploring the impact of the Gospel in different social contexts and on certain disadvantaged groups. Still, every theology, if it is not to become hopelessly abstract, is done in some context. With an emphasis on context, however, theology has become largely an interdisciplinary study.

For example, liberation theology draws on social and economic disciplines to uncover how the poor are disadvantaged by the structures of their societies. Feminist theology uses sociology and anthropology in its efforts to empower women. Postcolonial theology seeks to decolonize or deconstruct exclusively Western ways of knowing to recover the voices of marginalized groups and different cultures. Queer theology, appropriating a term too often used as an insult, works to empower members of the LGBTQ community. Eco-theology focuses on a care for the environment out of respect for God's gift of creation. Comparative theology puts Christianity in dialogue with other religious traditions, comparing one tradition on various points to another to gain a better understanding of both. All these different approaches represent efforts to learn from the different cultures and contexts in which Christians try to live out their discipleship.

The Pontifical Biblical Commission instruction on using the Bible in the church, mentioned earlier, also acknowledges the importance of contextual theologies. Noting that readers privilege some aspects of what they read and neglect others, the text points out that "some exegetes bring to their work points of view that are new and responsive to contemporary currents of thought which have not up till now been taken sufficiently into consideration. It is important that they do so with critical discernment." It then points to two examples. Liberation theology rightly emphasizes that God "is the God of the poor and cannot tolerate oppression or injustice." At the same time, it cautions against a one-sided approach, embracing a materialist analysis with a merely this-worldly eschatology or a Marxist view of the class struggle.

Turning toward a feminist biblical hermeneutic, it notes a variety of approaches, a radical form that denies all authority to the Bible, a neo-orthodox form that accepts the Bible as prophetic, and a critical form that seeks to uncover the status of women in the life of Jesus and the Pauline churches, often obscured by the patriarchy and androcentrism that developed later. Acknowledging the benefits that a feminist hermeneutic has brought to the position of women in the life of the church, it cautions against preconceived ideas that can lead to debatable interpretations of biblical texts. Still, it raises questions of power and its abuse in the church that can be useful today.

Some of these theologies build on Catholicism's carefully developed social teachings, beginning with Pope Leo XIII's famous 1891 encyclical, *Rerum Novarum*. Leo's encyclical criticized the idea that the marketplace should completely dominate the rights of working people, including the right to a living wage, to form protective associations or unions, and forbidding child labor. Subsequent popes have continued to develop this tradition, including teachings on international relations, war and peace, economic issues, the widening gap between the very rich and the poor, solidarity between peoples, the protection of human life, including that of the unborn, the death penalty, and the environment. Pope Francis has continued this tradition, drawing considerable opposition from some groups within the church.

Thus, the work of the Council remains unfinished. Some Catholics have been suspicious of the Council or have rejected it completely. To fully implement its reforms, Pope Francis has begun a synodal process, a "walking together" to allow all Catholics, clergy and laity, to reflect prayerfully on their shared ecclesial life. Still, pockets of opposition remain, with some against the very idea of change, especially some U.S. Catholics. Some have objected to Pope Francis's attempt to refocus Catholic moral concerns beyond the exclusive focus on abortion and same sex marriage. The pope has made his opposition to abortion clear, as is evident from his encyclical *Laudato Si'*. As he says, "how can we genuinely teach the importance of concern for other vulnerable beings, however troublesome or inconvenient they may be, if we fail to protect a human embryo, even when its presence is uncomfortable and creates difficulties?" (no. 120).

For other, affluent critics, their real problem is with Francis's economic teachings, his rejection in *Evangelii Gaudium* of what he calls an economy of exclusion and inequality, with its idolatry of money, its ideological defense of "trickle-down" economic theories that assumes that a free market will bring about greater justice and equality, an opinion that, he says, "has never been confirmed by facts (nos. 53–55).[10]

Pope Francis's efforts to address some of these issues, to create a more inclusive church by reaching out to those divorced and remarried, the LGBTQ community, or the concerns of women, have caused some Catholics, several cardinals among them, to accuse him of trying to change church doctrine, but there are several points to note here. Firstly, while dogmas are immutable, "irreformable" in official language, this is not true of all doctrines. There is a long history of official teachings that have changed over time. Examples include church teachings on slavery, religious liberty, usury, and the death penalty. Vatican II revised the teachings of earlier popes who denied that religious liberty or freedom of conscience was a fundamental human right, and it moved beyond the traditional *extra ecclesia, nulla salus*, no salvation outside the church, as well as Pope Pius XII's exclusive identification of the Mystical Body of Christ with the Catholic Church.[11]

Secondly, a pope cannot change doctrine by himself; his role is to reflect and safeguard the faith of the church, and to do so he must be sensitive to the *sensus fidei* and the *sensus fidelium*, the sense of faith and sense of the faithful.[12] Francis has said he is not trying to change doctrine, but he is trying to change people's attitudes on some of these disputed issues, to make them more open and welcoming toward those who find it difficult to live out the fullness of Catholic teachings in their own lives. Changing attitudes may lead eventually to the development of doctrine.

It is also true, as we have seen, that many no longer walk with the church. In a secular age, many others have become "disaffiliated" from their churches, mosques, and synagogues, joining the "nones." The church needs to find ways to renew its evangelical mission, to find a new language to communicate the riches of the Gospel. Its moral theology, too long focused on sin, needs renewal, especially on sexuality.[13] The church's teachings on homosexuality seem to many out of date, no longer congruent with what we know today about sexual orientation as a given, rather than the more traditional language of sexual preference.

The church struggles to find more ways to include those in the LGBTQ community, and it has yet to recognize fully the gifts of women, and how they might contribute even more to the life of the church. Pope Francis has already taken significant steps in this direction. In April 2023, the Vatican announced that seventy nonbishops—priests, deacons, religious, and laypeople—would participate with the right to vote in the October Synod on Synodality, with at least half of them women. The magisterium's teaching on why women cannot be ordained is not convincing to many, and the question has never been openly considered, using the fullness of the church's resources, its theologians and historians, its sense of the faithful, and its bishops.

There are other challenges as well. Conservative Christianity in the United States has too often reduced the Gospel to a narrowly individualistic doctrine of salvation, an "I got saved" approach that ignores the Gospels' social dimensions. The Catholic Church has a rich tradition of teachings on social justice, but those teachings are not always evident in the response of so many Catholics to problems such as white supremacy and racism that remains embedded in much of American culture. Migration is another problem; millions of migrants are fleeing poverty, violence, and persecution today, as they seek better lives for their families. So is the ecological crisis that threatens the health of our beautiful earth. All these problems stand as challenges to our discipleship.

Conclusion

Although many people today, less schooled in the diverse ways of knowing, believe that religion and science are antithetical, such an attitude is foreign to the Catholic tradition. Catholics are not biblical fundamentalists, and they take for granted the complementarity of faith and reason.

The Second Vatican Council's Dogmatic Constitution on Divine Revelation (*Dei Verbum*) put Scripture back at the center of Catholic theology and life. In teaching that God's revelation finds its fullness in the person of Jesus the Christ, it moved beyond a literalist or propositional understanding of Scripture. Revelation is more than a text. It is personal, christological, and often symbolic. It needs critical interpretation.

From early Christian history, evangelists and theologians have sought to learn from the wisdom of their encompassing cultures. Although there have been some embarrassing exceptions, this has also been true of contemporary Catholic scholars. Plato's thought long served as a framework for theology, especially in the work of Augustine and others in his tradition. In the thirteenth century, influenced by the Dominican Thomas Aquinas, many medieval thinkers turned to the works of Aristotle for the same reason.

While the problem of suffering remains not just a mystery but a serious objection to belief in God's existence, an inadequate theodicy leads many to see God falsely as complacent in the face of evil, if not responsible for it. A deeper theology understands God as respecting the freedom of his creatures, renouncing coercive power while continuing to work deep within the evolutionary process, drawing creation to its ultimate fulfillment in himself.

The list of Catholic scientists, astronomers, and mathematicians is lengthy, from Hildegard of Bingen in the twelfth century to Guy Consolmagno today. Catholic theology, once freed from the confines of a nonhistorical Neo-Scholasticism, has tried to both learn from culture and transform it. Historical and literary studies have transformed our understanding of the Bible and the church's tradition. Contextual theologies, many of them drawing on other disciplines, have sought to bring the Gospel's light to disadvantaged groups, our human experience, and the earth itself. Vatican II, besides its efforts to renew the church and its mission, for the first time brought lay men and women into the task of theology, introducing new voices that soon transformed the discipline.

Yet the Council's renewal of Catholic life remains incomplete. Pope Francis has challenged the churches to learn how to walk together in a synodal process and listen to each other. There has been some opposition from those who fear change, but most have welcomed his efforts.

4

Encountering the Divine Mystery

CHRISTIAN FAITH DOES not begin with some form of message, with words from heaven or a doctrine. It begins with an *experience*. So says the great Belgian Dominican Edward Schillebeeckx at the beginning of his *Interim Report* on his two volumes on Christology. His point was that certain people who encountered Jesus came to experience redemption, liberation, a new life experience. As they began to communicate this experience to others, their experience became a message.

Schillebeeckx stresses that to proclaim Jesus the Christ is not a matter of handing on doctrine; "grace and salvation, redemption and religion, need not be expressed in strange, 'supernatural' terms: they can be put into ordinary human language, the language of encounter and experience, above all the language of picture and image, testimony and story, never detached from a specific liberating event."[1] This does not mean that doctrine is unimportant; doctrine is the later interpretation of that experience, brought to expression in language, carefully formulated, and handed on in what became the church's living tradition. The *Directory for Catechesis* makes the same point: "Evangelization is not, in the first place, the delivery of a doctrine; but rather, making present and announcing Jesus Christ."[2] Christian faith has its beginning in this inner experience of the disciples.

This is also the approach of Pope Francis. In his 2013 apostolic exhortation *Evangelii Gaudium*, he stresses the importance of "popular piety" in which the Gospel becomes inculturated, especially for the poor: "We should not think…that the Gospel message must always be communicated by fixed formulations learned by heart or by specific words which express an absolutely invariable content. This communication takes place in so many different ways that it would be impossible to describe or catalogue them all" (no. 129).

Signs and Wonders

This is not always easy for people. So many of us want evidence, proof, especially something dramatic. The apostle Thomas, called the "Doubter," was not able to believe in the resurrection until the risen Jesus invited him to probe his wounds with his finger and put his hand into the wound in his side. Dramatic evidence for sure, but the passage is most probably not an historical report, but a story written by the evangelist to bring other followers of Jesus to Easter faith, as is clear from what Jesus says to Thomas: "Have you come to believe because you have seen me? Blessed are those who have not seen and have believed" (John 20:29). Shortly after his election to the papacy, Pope Francis expressed a healthy skepticism about claims of healings, revelations, and visions, saying that God is not like Federal Express, sending us messages all the time. The real tests of supernatural phenomena, he says, are "simplicity, humility and the absence of a spectacle."[3]

This is not to deny that what theologians call the "Easter Experience" of the earliest disciples brought them to faith in his resurrection, the conviction that he was still present with them, but not as he was during his historical ministry. The resurrection should not be understood as an objective this-worldly event, to be reported with the news announcement, "film at eleven." It was not simply an "objective" event, observable to any potential observer. Nor was it subjective, in the sense of something only in the minds of the disciples. The resurrection was a transhistorical or eschatological event, an event on the far side of time and history. It was real in that it happened to a real person. The risen Jesus now lives fully in God's presence. We can understand it, even if we cannot imagine it.

It was also real, and transformative to those to whom Jesus revealed himself, to those who loved him and were open to his risen presence. Jesus did not appear to those whose hearts were closed to him. We don't know exactly the nature of the disciples' Easter experience, whether it was visual, imaginative, or something they experienced interiorly, but history tells us that these frightened men and women, regathered and hiding in the upper room had, by the end of the century, established churches through much of the known world.

Still, there is something mysterious about the Easter appearances. These stories suggest that the Twelve and other disciples themselves had to be brought to Easter faith. Read the appearance stories carefully. When Jesus makes his risen presence known to the disciples, they are frightened or bewildered; they fail to recognize him or think they are seeing a ghost. In Matthew, even as Jesus appeared to them on the mountain in Galilee, some continue to doubt (28:17). Perhaps these disciples also wanted something more dramatic or demonstrative, but faith or belief in Jesus is always a free response to a movement in our spirits, to God's call that touches us in some way. God does not force us to believe; God always respects our freedom.

The New Testament constantly warns us about making belief contingent on signs and wonders. Even during Jesus's ministry, people were slow to believe; they wanted something more dramatic. To the royal official, he says, "Unless you people see signs and wonders, you will not believe" (John 4:48). The Pharisees and Sadducees wanted a sign from heaven (cf. Mark 8:11–12; Matt 16:1–4). Jesus warns his disciples: "False messiahs and false prophets will arise, and they will perform signs and wonders so great as to deceive, if that were possible, even the elect" (Matt 24:24). Even after his *resurrection*, he says to the two disciples on the road to Emmaus, "Oh, how foolish you are! How slow of heart to believe all that the prophets spoke" (Luke 24:25). Paul tells the Corinthians, "Jews demand signs and Greeks look for wisdom" (1 Cor 1:22).

Nor are we so different. Many Catholics remain fascinated by the dramatic or the supernatural, with miraculous objects—weeping statues, rosaries turned to gold, bleeding hosts, the miraculously preserved bodies of the saints, apparitions of Jesus and his mother—taking them as evidence for their faith. Respecting popular religion and the need to find cultural expressions of the faith, the Catholic Church is tolerant of some of these, but they remain optional. They are not matters of faith. Most conservative Protestants see biblical stories as infallible, historically true.

So, how do we encounter the God whose very otherness transcends our senses and blinds our intellect? As God remains transcendent, our encounter with the divine is always mediated in some way, by nature or our imaginations, by words, symbols, or ritual action, by experiences of love or compassion or insight.

We can sense the mystery of the Triune God in our own experience, if indirectly. We experience God as transcendent but at the same time intimate and close. We come to know Jesus by contemplating the Gospel stories and reaching out to others in need. The Spirit frequently moves our hearts, filling them with joy, moving us closer to God. While we can gain some sense of Father, Son, and Spirit in their distinctive missions, as theology would describe it, we should not think that the three "persons" are three independent selves or subjectivities, persons in the modern psychological sense. The church has long used the language of three "persons" as a form of grammar, suggesting how God turns in love toward us as well as the relationality at the very heart of the divine.⁴ We need to consider this mystery more closely.

God

At the beginning of his *Spiritual Exercises*, St. Ignatius of Loyola proposes an exercise called the "First Principle and Foundation." He tells the retreatant that we are created to praise, reverence, and serve God, and by this means to save our souls. All other created things are to help us attain this end. The language is rather dated; Ignatius is writing in the Christian culture of the sixteenth century. He suggests that we make ourselves "indifferent" to all created things. A better way of expressing this would be encouraging the retreatant to strive for "spiritual freedom," so important in the spiritual life, and for a retreat.

For God speaks in silence. While God in his mercy sometimes breaks through the clutter of our imaginations, it is difficult to encounter God when we are caught up in desiring things that are finally inconsequential. As Pope Benedict once said in a sermon, "God is not loud. He does not make headlines."⁵ We need to listen carefully. We need to be attentive, clear away the distractions that so often fill our imaginations, practice that inner awareness that Buddhists call mindfulness, but if God does not encounter us in the dramatic, in signs and wonders, that does not mean that God does not touch our hearts and make his presence known. As we saw at the beginning of this chapter, God touches us in our inner experience.

There is a wonderful story in the First Book of Kings. The prophet Elijah, fleeing from his enemies, takes shelter in a cave. Close to despair, he hears God telling him to stand outside on the mountain because "the LORD will be passing by" (1 Kgs 19:11). He watches as a strong wind buffets the mountain, crushing rocks before it, but God was not in the wind. Next came an earthquake, but the Lord was not in the earthquake. Then there was fire, but the

Lord was not in the fire. Finally, he heard a tiny whispering sound, and when he heard this, "Elijah hid his face in his cloak."

The story suggests the transcendence or otherness of God. God is not a being or object in the world to be observed and studied as the new atheists seem to suggest. God is pure subsistent being, *ipsum esse subsistens* as Aquinas argues, not able to be grasped by our finite intellects. Trying to understand God is like staring into the sun. We must use metaphors and symbols. Our efforts to imagine or understand the divine always fall short. God remains mystery.

When we consider that those responsible for the Hebrew Scriptures came from a primitive people, herding their sheep and goats before settling into a more agrarian life in Palestine, the image of God that emerges in their literature is so different from that of their neighbors. Israel's God, although close to his people, is holy, other, transcendent. The Book of Exodus describes God as hidden in an impenetrable cloud (Exod 20:21; 24:15). The Decalogue forbade the Israelites from attempting to represent God by means of images (Exod 20:4; cf. Deut 5:8). The psalmist mocks the pagans for their worship, based on bloody sacrifices: "Were I hungry, I would not tell you, for mine is the world and all that fills it. Do I eat the flesh of bulls or drink the blood of goats?" (Ps 50:12–13). Or he mocks his people for their idolatry: "At Horeb they fashioned a calf, worshiped a metal statue. They exchanged their glorious God for the image of a grass-eating bull" (Ps 106:19–20). The God of Israel is a compassionate God: "You, Lord, are a merciful and gracious God, slow to anger, most loving and true" (Ps 86:15).

There is an ethical dimension to their relationship with Yahweh. Their God is holy and demands that his people act justly. "You have been told, O man, what is good, and what the LORD requires of you: Only to do the right and to love goodness, and to walk humbly with your God" (Mic 6:8). Exodus reminds the people that God hears the cry of the poor (Exod 22:26). The very terms of God's covenant with Israel are ethical precepts, the Ten Commandments or Decalogue. God alone is to be honored. They are to abstain from idolatry, not take the Lord's name in vain, keep the Sabbath holy, and honor their parents. They shall not kill, commit adultery, steal, or bear false witness against a neighbor or covet their goods. Still less should they take part in the orgiastic fertility rites of their neighbors.

In the Christian tradition, the metaphors of darkness and light are used to portray the otherness of the divine. The author of 1 Timothy describes God as dwelling in unapproachable light (1 Tim 6:16). Gregory of Nyssa speaks paradoxically of God hidden in "luminous darkness." Anselm speaks of God as dwelling in an inaccessible light that blinds the intellect:

> Surely, Lord, inaccessible light is your dwelling place, for no one apart from yourself can enter into it and fully comprehend you. If I fail to see this light, it is simply because it is too bright for me. Still, it is by this light that I do see all that I can, even as weak eyes, unable to look straight at the sun, see all that can be seen by the sun's light.

A famous fourteenth-century mystical work encourages its readers to approach God, not by considering God's activities or attributes, but by abiding in a *Cloud of Unknowing*, the title of the work. We encounter God when we open ourselves in silent prayer. This is the apophatic approach that has inspired so many mystics. If God is transcendent, a blinding light to our limited intellects, then how can we know anything about God. As the author of the Fourth Gospel says, "No one has ever seen God. The only Son, God, who is at the Father's side, has revealed him" (John 1:18), but even the revealing word can be only a partial disclosure. God remains mystery.

Karl Rahner, in his later years, spoke increasingly about the incomprehensibility (*Unbegreiflichkeit*) of God, by which he meant our inability to fully understand or grasp the divine mystery. Even if our intellect constantly moves beyond what it grasps, God remains beyond our intellect's ability to comprehend, but as he says in his

Foundations of Christian Faith, we are oriented toward mystery, toward God, "this unthematic and ever-present experience, this knowledge of God which we always have even when we are thinking of and concerned with anything but God, is the permanent ground from out of which thematic knowledge of God emerges."[6] The Catholic tradition holds that we can affirm God's existence on the basis of reason, but if we are to know God in any particular way, we are dependent on revelation, on God's free self-disclosure.

Rahner suggests something more, an intuition of the divine mystery or orientation that structures the very nature of our understanding. Like Aquinas, Rahner sees a kinship between the human intellect and God toward which it is oriented. As Aquinas says, our human intellect "is nothing more than a participating likeness of the uncreated light."[7]

Scripture opens with the story of God's creation of the heavens and the earth, the living creatures that fill the earth, the plants that decorate it, and most of all, the man and woman who will populate it, but God's creative work is not done. All too often, we imagine creation as something done in the past, but God's creative work is ongoing, a *creatio continua* or continuing creation. Elizabeth Johnson speaks of a "beloved community of creation." "In creating the world, God is present here and now to each creature, loving each into existence and promising its future. When trouble comes, God does not abandon the beloved creature."[8] Creation itself is radically contingent, dependent on God's sustaining grace. If God were to withdraw it, we and all that is would in a moment cease to exist. Although of course, God is not in time; time is only the measure of movements in the created order. As Roger Haight says, "Creation…does not refer to temporal beginning but to the relationship of all finite being to its source and ground of being."[9]

Thus, the transcendent God is also immanent to creation, another instance of the Catholic tendency to say "both/and." The transcendent God is nearer to us than we are to ourselves. Catholic theology with its sacramental imagination sees God's presence in all things, working, sustaining, giving life, sensation, and understanding, reflecting God's goodness and beauty, as St. Ignatius invites the retreatant to contemplate in the *Contemplatio ad amorem*.[10] St. Augustine saw this clearly, as he wrote with his poetic imagination in his famous *Confessions*:

> Late have I loved you, O Beauty ever ancient, ever new, late have I loved you! You were within me, but I was outside, and it was there that I searched for you. In my unloveliness I plunged into the lovely things which you created. You were with me, but I was not with you. Created things kept me from you; yet if they had not been in you they would have not been at all.[11]

God is indeed present in creation, but still distinct from it. Unlike the first Genesis account of Creation, the ancient Mesopotamian myth, on which it was based, saw creation as the result of a cosmic battle between Marduk, the god of the Babylonians and Tiamat, a monster serpent goddess representing the primeval watery chaos.[12] The first Genesis account shows a literary dependence on the early story. Both accounts are mythical, but they are entirely different. In the Genesis account (Gen 1:1—2:4a), there is no cosmogony. God creates effortlessly by the sovereign power of the divine word, bringing cosmic order and design by dividing the primeval chaos. Later theological reflection will take a step further, teaching *creatio ex nihilo*, a creation from nothing in recognition of the continuing absolute dependence of all things on God's creative power.

If the first creation story is mythical, however, it has an important truth to teach. Creation is the work of God's hands, and it is good. The man and woman are created in the image and likeness of God, and hence have an intrinsic dignity. The Genesis story and science are not in conflict. Science tells us how the universe and vast array of species came to be; the biblical account speaks of its ultimate cause or source. These are different ways of knowing, and both have much to teach us.

So does the story of the fall in Genesis chapter 3 and following chapters. Its message makes clear that evil does not come from the creator but from the human beings falling for the serpent's temptation, inviting them to become like gods themselves, thus failing to acknowledge the creator. The result is that the chaos God overcame at the beginning rushes back into the ordered cosmos; in the following chapters, brother kills brother, creation itself is threatened in the story of the flood, and finally comes the "confusing" of languages, the story of the tower of Babel, the result of human pride.

The opening chapters of Genesis show us a humankind damaged and in need of God's grace, God's salvation. From this idea, Augustine was to develop his theology of original sin, but original sin is not like a defective gene, passed on through marital intercourse. It is not primarily a biological concept, but a radically social one. Born into a sinful world, we are affected by it. Our families are often dysfunctional; our societies self-centered and polarized, putting self-interests first; our cultures carry embedded prejudices against those who are different, racially, sexually, economically. Unlike Protestant theology, however, which from the Reformers on sees human nature as "totally depraved," with intellect constrained and the will having been corrupted, Catholic theological anthropology is more positive. It sees nature as damaged but also graced. God's creation is good; it is never without grace. Another example of the Catholic both/and.

The transcendent God often makes us aware of his presence. We often sense it in the beauty of nature, in the warmth of the sun, the cool breeze rippling the meadow, or the night sky filled with stars. Nature itself is like a sacrament, the first book of revelation. God's presence is comforting; it is sustaining and life-giving. Life itself in all its profusion and exuberance suggests the munificence of its Creator, in the sparrow hopping happily outside my door, the joy on the face of a child, or the warmth of a lover's embrace. In moments like this, we find God's presence in the ordinary, filling us with peace. Yet having this sense for God's presence often makes us long for more; we have been touched, awakened. We find ourselves breaking out in praise.

Occasionally, God draws us into a dark silence, quieting our busy senses. As Thomas Merton writes, "You may find that you can rest in this darkness and this unfathomable peace without trouble and without anxiety, even when the imagination and the mind remain in some way active outside the doors of it. They may stand and chatter in the porch, as long as they are idle, waiting for the will of their queen to return, upon whose order they depend."[13] In these moments, we feel God's presence, giving us a deep sense of peace. In trying to express the inexpressible in their writing, mystics often compare it to the conjugal embrace. There is deep comfort in these moments.

Jesus

Jesus's presence can be more challenging. As an historical figure who walked this earth, Jesus has both a body and a voice. Neither is difficult to find. We find his voice in the Gospels and his body in the church.

A Galilean from Nazareth, of the house of David, Jesus exercised a brief preaching ministry and was known as a wonderworker. Because of his threat to the Roman rule of Judah and out of jealousy on the part of some of the Jewish leaders, he was put to a shameful death by crucifixion. The Jewish historian Josephus in his *Antiquities of the Jews* (c. 93–94 CE) gives the clearest extrabiblical witness to Jesus's life and ministry, after some later Christian additions were removed. Here is a critical reconstruction of the text:

> Now there was about this time Jesus, a wise man. For he was a doer of startling deeds, a teacher of such men as receive the truth with pleasure. And he gained a following

both among many Jews and many of Greek origin. And when Pilate, at the suggestion of the principal men amongst us, condemned him to the cross, those that loved him at the first did not forsake him. And the tribe of Christians, so named from him, are not extinct at this day.

Josephus also refers to John the Baptist in his work, and there are some brief references to Jesus and his fate from other early sources. Tacitus (c. 116), a Roman senator and historian, refers to his death under Pontius Pilate, and to his followers who Nero blamed for the great fire in Rome. The Roman historian Suetonius (69–122) seems to refer to early Christians he holds responsible for a disturbance in Rome, although in referring to Jesus he misspells his name as Chrestus. According to Gerhard Lohfink, the Jewish Babylonian Talmud also has a polemical reference to Jesus that reads: "[Jesus] practiced magic and led Israel astray."[14]

While we are familiar with the story of Jesus from the four canonical Gospels, they were addressed to early Christian communities and written in light of the resurrection. Thus, while containing historical material, they represent early Christian preaching. As Elizabeth Johnson points out, for much of the Christian tradition, Christology was summarized in terms of his miraculous birth and his death,[15] with additional attention to the resurrection, church, and Pentecost event. Think of the creeds, with their trinitarian confession of faith, concluding with reference to the resurrection, the forgiveness of sins, the church, and the resurrection of the body. The Rosary is similar. Its mysteries invite us to contemplate prayerfully the annunciation and visitation, Jesus's birth and two temple events, the passion, resurrection, gift of the Spirit, and two of the Marian mysteries, but what this approach overlooks is the actual ministry and teaching of Jesus, especially his preaching about the reign of God.

Pope John Paul II wisely addressed this oversight by adding the "Luminous Mysteries" to the Rosary.[16] Yet it was the long "search for the historical Jesus" that provided such an important recovery of the actual ministry of Jesus, both for Christology and for Christian faith and discipleship. Without it, we would not have had the clear focus on the social dimensions of Jesus preaching, especially the reign of God, the Beatitudes, the Lord's Prayer, and his concern for the poor and the disadvantaged (cf. Matt 25:31–46). Historical-critical scholarship has recovered a portrait of the historical Jesus, giving us greater appreciation of the development of the Gospel tradition, and helping us hear again the actual voice of Jesus.

As the Pontifical Biblical Commission taught in its *Instruction on the Historical Truth of the Gospels*, the Gospels went through a development from the original words and deeds of Jesus, the oral preaching of the early Christian communities, and their actual writing by the evangelists, over a period of some seventy years.

From the first stage we learn how Jesus spoke and taught in his historical ministry. We hear his voice clearly in his calling God "Abba," in his parables, and in his sayings. For the Jews, God's personal name was Yahweh, a name so holy that faithful Jews would not even pronounce it, but we know that Jesus addressed God with the word *abba*, an intimate term for one's father used by sons and daughters within the closeness of the family or home. Using such familiar language for God was foreign to the Jewish tradition of his time. While the prophets sometimes refer to Yahweh as the Father of Israel, we can find in the Hebrew Scriptures no example of a Jew speaking to God in such familiar fashion. Jesus's use of the term certainly says something about how he understood his own relation to God. He also referred to himself as the "Son."

We also hear the voice of Jesus in the parables, short stories illustrative of some point that characterized Jesus's teaching. Most of us can think of a parable we particularly cherish, for example, the prodigal son, the good Samaritan, the sower and the seed, the pearl of great price, the rich man and Lazarus, the pharisee and the tax collector, and so on. One of my favorites is the workers in the vineyard (Matt 20:1–16). In the parable, a landowner begins at dawn to hire laborers to work in his field, but at the end of the day when he gathers the workers to pay them for their labors, he pays those who came at the last hour just as much as those who worked all day. Although I used to think the parable was unfair—paying all the laborers equally rather they considering how long each had worked—it is rich in meaning. It challenged me. God is not like us; God's standards are different, not *quid pro quo*, but an incredible generosity. My students always point out that one can be saved, even at the last minute. While true, there may be some self-interest there.

The parable also suggests God's special concern for the poor. When the landowner goes out at 5:00 in the evening and sees some "standing around" and questions them, they respond, "no one has hired us." They and their families depend on their employment, but they are still waiting. That verse reminds me of the huge building supply store in our neighborhood. It always has a line of workers waiting for the contractors in their pickups to hire them, even at the end of the day. Jesus tells us that we encounter him in the poor (cf. Matt 25:1–16). This has long been the experience of those like St. Teresa of Calcutta and others dedicated to supporting the sick, the hungry, and the suffering. They see the face of Jesus in the face of those for whom they care.

Jesus's parables have this wonderful quality of raising difficult questions, making us think. So often they are taken from ordinary life, stories of travelers and farmers, rich guests at wedding feasts and the poor and hungry outside, as well as landlords, laborers, and dishonest administrators. They challenge us to see things differently. As Eamonn Bredin says, there is something shocking and subversive about the parables of Jesus: "It is the *Samaritan* who is neighbor, it is the *last* who are first, it is the *lost* who are rejoiced over, the *stranger* who is at table, the *wastrel* son who is embraced and fêted."[17]

We also hear the voice of Jesus in his *logia* or sayings. While the Gospels contain many of the sayings of Jesus, many come from what scholars call "Q" (from the German *Quelle* or "source"), a collection of his sayings used by Matthew and Luke in their Gospels but not by

Mark. Q may have been a text, or at least an oral collection of sayings; some scholars speak of the Q community. Especially important among the sayings are the Beatitudes, the Sermon on the Mount or on the Plain, and the Lord's Prayer. The Lord's Prayer has become the most familiar Christian prayer that stems from Jesus himself.

The sayings give us insight into the tone and tenor of Jesus's preaching. Some Christians tend to domesticate his language, eliminating any sayings that are particularly challenging or have a hard edge, giving us the "easy Jesus," but the sayings are indeed challenging. The Beatitudes offer a description of the qualities that should describe the disciples, but they also suggest Jesus's special love for the poor, the hungry, and the suffering. He calls on his disciples to be peace makers, to have clean hearts, to be willing to endure persecution for the sake of the kingdom of heaven. They should be willing to take the last place; those in authority should consider themselves as servants.

His sayings are similar. Jesus calls for conversion, or better, for a *metanoia* or radical change of heart: "There is nothing outside a person that by going in can defile, but the things that come out are what defile" (Mark 7:15), or "Love your enemies and pray for those who persecute you" (Matt 5:44). Becoming his disciple entails some struggle, as in "whoever wishes to save his life will lose it, but whoever loses his life for my sake and that of the gospel will save it" (Mark 8:35). The idea of a final reversal of status occurs in many of his sayings, as in "many that are first will be last, and the last first" (Matt 19:30), and "whoever exalts himself will be humbled, and whoever humbles himself will be exalted" (Matt 23:12). He warns about the danger of wealth: "It is easier for a camel to go through the eye of a needle than for a rich man to enter the kingdom of God" (Matt 19:24). Most of all, he proclaims the coming of the kingdom of God: "No one who sets his hand to the plow and looks back is fit for the kingdom of God" (Luke 9:62), and "Truly, I say to you, whoever does not receive the kingdom of God like a child shall not enter it" (Mark 10:15). These are just a few of his authentic sayings.[18]

TO BELIEVE OR NOT BELIEVE

Yet Jesus is more than an ethical teacher. To reduce to ethical precepts what the New Testament or Christianity itself teaches about Jesus is to collapse the Christian mystery into a mere moralism. All too often, this is the mistake of liberal theology. Christianity is so much more, and so much more personal. As Pope Benedict said at the beginning of his first encyclical, *Deus Caritas Est*, "Being Christian is not the result of an ethical choice or a lofty idea, but the encounter with an event, a person, which gives life a new horizon and a decisive direction" (no. 1).

As we saw at the beginning of this chapter, we encounter Jesus, not in signs and wonders, but in our inner experience, inviting him into our lives. Scripture gives us many examples of how we do this. Here are just a few. He tells us in Revelation, "Listen! I am standing at the door, knocking; if you hear my voice and open the door, I will come in to you and eat with you, and you with me" (Rev 3:20). In Matthew, he says, "Not everyone who says to me, 'Lord, Lord,' will enter the kingdom of heaven, but only the one who does the will of my Father in heaven" (Matt 7:21). In John, he tells us, "Whoever loves me will be loved by my Father, and I will love him and reveal myself to him" (John 14:21). Importantly, he says, "Peace I leave with you; my peace I give to you" (John 14:27). So often we know Christ's presence within us by a quiet peace, a sense of being at home despite the chaos that often marks our daily lives; we sense that God is not distant from us.

Edward Schillebeeckx expressed this most basic truth of Christianity when he entitled one of his books *Christ the Sacrament of the Encounter with God*, for in Jesus we encounter the divine mystery, we come to the God who loves us passionately, for he is God become one of us.

The New Testament seeks to express this mystery using metaphorical language. St. Paul speaks of Jesus as the image or icon (*eikōn*) of God (cf. 2 Cor 4:4; Col 1:15). When Philip asks Jesus to show the Father to the disciples, Jesus replies, "Have I been with you for so long a time and you still do not know me, Philip? Whoever has seen me has seen the Father" (John 14:9). So too, we who bear the image of the first Adam "will also bear the image of the man of heaven" (1 Cor 15:49). This is Christ's salvific work, forgiving us our sins, restoring our ability to image God and reflect God's glory (cf. 1 Cor 11:7), and drawing us to the Father. It took some time for the Church to develop its Christology in more conceptual language, as we shall see in the next chapter when we consider the fullness of God's salvation.

The Spirit

The Spirit of God or the Holy Spirit is more obscure conceptually but more directly experienced. We experience the Spirit's presence interiorly, in our hearts. As Brian Daley says, "The Spirit does the work of God but seems to lack a 'face'—a *prosopon*; the Spirit is a gift, a force, but seems not to have the individual concreteness that Greek philosophy refers to by the term *hypostasis*."[19] The Spirit is felt rather than easily imagined. When the Spirit moves us, we sense God's presence.

The Old Testament speaks of the Spirit as the wind or spirit of God. The spirit sweeps over the waters at creation (Gen 1:2) and inspires the prophets. God's spirit will be poured out on all people in the messianic age. (cf. Ezek 36:26; Joel 3:1–2). Jesus is conceived by the Holy Spirit; it descends on him at his baptism in the Jordan (Mark 1:10) and leads him into the wilderness where he is tempted (Luke 4:1). Luke sees his ministry as empowered by the Spirit, and after his resurrection the Spirit is poured out upon the apostles, to guide them in their ministry of evangelizing and founding churches (Acts 2:41).

Paul speaks of the risen Christ as "a life-giving spirit" (1 Cor 15:45). To be "in Christ" is to have new life "in the Spirit." Notice how Paul points to the Spirit's work in our subjectivity or affectivity. The Spirit is the source of our faith; it enables us to confess Jesus as

Lord (cf. 1 Cor 12:3) and to call on God as Abba (cf. Rom 8:15). His language here is powerful; the Spirit pours the love of God into our hearts (cf. Rom 5:5), giving us a sense of our kinship with the transcendent God and an awareness of ourselves as beloved sons and daughters, able to call on God as our Abba also, just as the early Christians did. Similarly, the Spirit's grace effects a transformation of our own spirits. Paul writes that the "fruit of the Spirit is love, joy, peace, patience, kindness, generosity, faithfulness, gentleness, self-control" (Gal 5:22–23). The Spirit and grace are virtually synonymous; both refer to God's presence in our hearts, and because that presence is abiding, God is never distant from us. We can encounter him within if we open ourselves to his grace. The Spirit abides within us, in our affectivity and in our hearts. Jesus encourages his disciples to ask the Father for the gift of the Spirit (cf. Luke 11:13).

Both Paul and John highlight the Spirit's role in the life of the church. The Spirit is the source of unity, bringing Jews and Greeks together into one body (cf. 1 Cor 12:13), the body of Christ. The church is "the household of God...a dwelling place of God in the Spirit" (Eph 2:20, 22). The very structure of the church is charismatic, with the Spirit pouring out a diversity of gifts and ministries (cf. 1 Cor 12:4–6). John says that the Spirit or Advocate sent from the Father "will teach you all things...that I have said to you" (John 14:26). Thus, for John also, the Spirit continues to guide the community of disciples, the church. We need to consider the church more carefully.

The Church

The Church is the Body of Christ, a metaphor first used by Paul. During his historical life, Jesus gathered a group of disciples who shared his itinerant ministry and learned from his example and his parables, but being a disciple of Jesus was different from being a disciple of the Pharisees. The disciples of Jesus did not join his group or "movement," as it is called by scholars today, on their own initiative, but were invited by Jesus, called personally. His movement was inclusive; not limited to the ritually pure or the religiously observant; Jesus called ordinary men, workers, perhaps some politically involved like Simon the Zealot, as well as "tax collectors and sinners" (Mark 2:15), for which he was frequently criticized. He broke with the culture of the time by also calling women. Most importantly, unlike the disciples of the rabbis whose task was to learn their teaching, the disciples of Jesus shared in his ministry. Jesus sent them out to proclaim that the reign of God is at hand, to cure the sick, cleanse lepers, and drive out demons (cf. Luke 9:1–2; Matt 10:7–8). His movement became the Church.

In a very early letter to the church at Corinth written around the year 51, Paul tells the Corinthian Christians that they are one body, united by baptism (cf. 1 Cor 12:13) and by sharing in the cup of blessing and broken bread of the Eucharist. "Because the loaf of bread is one, we, though many, are one body, for we all partake of the one loaf" (1 Cor 10:17). The later church would call these sacraments.

Far from teaching justification by faith alone, Paul's letters are all to or about churches. To be "in Christ" is to be in his body, the church. It is the Christian community, in its teaching and sacraments, its charisms and ministries, its worship and community that mediates the presence of the risen Jesus; the church makes Christ visible. Without it, how would we come to know him? While the church has institutional elements, it is not primarily an institution; it is a community of faith.

We encounter God in Scripture and sacrament. We acknowledge Scripture as God's word, although Protestant Christians, raised on the Bible, often have a better sense of this. Yet Catholics also reverence Scripture. Vatican II placed it again at the center of Catholic catechetics, theology, worship, and spirituality. Sacramental moments frequently mediate an experience of God. Many find a new relationship with God in baptism. Penance can bring a deep sense of healing and reconciliation, while the sacrament of the sick or viaticum, strengthens the Christian for the final journey or brings healing. The love of spouses in marriage can mirror for each an experience God's love. Catholics see themselves encountering the risen Jesus especially in the Eucharist, which incorporates them into his body, the church.

Many today ask why we need the Church. All too often, the problem is with the Church itself. As one research team noted, the distance from God is less than the distance from the Church. Some are put off by the sins of Christians and the failure of the Church to deal with them. The sexual abuse scandal has been particularly damaging. Others are suspicious of institutions in general. They find the Church—or better, churchmen—too judgmental. Catholic priests are not generally known for the quality of their preaching, while the current shortage of priests means that parishes in the United States are increasingly dependent on foreign-born priests, mostly from Africa and India. While many are fine pastors, their heavily accented English means that many American Catholics have difficulty understanding their preaching. Some bishops have reduced the church's concern to being against abortion and same-sex marriage. Pope Francis has challenged Catholics to take a broader perspective, a more inclusive vision.

Catholic teaching is a much more comprehensive reality. Important as doctrine is, Catholic teaching is more than its doctrine. As Pope Francis states, "All revealed truths derive from the same divine source and are to be believed with the same faith, yet some of them are more important for giving direct expression to the heart of the Gospel. In this basic core, what shines forth is the beauty of the saving love of God made manifest in Jesus Christ who died and rose from the dead" (EG 36). The church loses this when it focuses only on doctrine, or on the culture wars. The church has a rich body of social teaching; the social dimensions of the Gospel cannot be ignored. We are radically social creatures, not autonomous individuals. Just as sin is mediated socially, so too is grace. We cannot be a Christian in solitary isolation.

We come to know the Lord Jesus in the community of his disciples, living in the grace of the Holy Spirit. Francis's emphasis on synodality is a recognition that the Spirit is active in the whole church, not just in the hierarchy.[20] He has strongly reclaimed the neglected doctrines of the *sensus fidei* and the *sensus fidelium* ("sense of the faith" and "sense of the faithful"); the faithful are not merely passive recipients of hierarchical teaching but active subjects who play a role in the development of doctrine, even in its moral teaching.[21]

We encounter the risen Christ in the sacraments, especially the Eucharist, receiving him intimately in holy communion, as the Council of Trent taught, "body and blood, soul and divinity." But grace-filled liturgies need more than solid theological foundations; they need homilies that speak to people's real concerns and touch their hearts, a music ministry that draws them into the worship, and welcoming congregations. The Scriptures need an interpreting community if they are to be rightly understood. The fractured body of Christ today, divided into so many disparate denominations, is witness to the surfeit of private interpretation.

As the body of Christ, the church makes Jesus present and visible to the world. My friend Terrence Tilley says, where would Jesus be without his body, the church? It enables others to encounter him. It proclaims him in its preaching and teaching, celebrates him in its liturgy, ministers in his name to vast numbers, and gathers them in communion with disciples around the world. The great missionary movement that began for the Catholic Church after the so-called discovery of the new worlds of Africa, Asia, and the Americas has largely been transformed into social ministries and interreligious dialogue. While in its respect for the religious other, the Church has moved beyond proselytization, in fidelity to the church's evangelical mission, Christians still strive to witness to the Gospel at home and abroad.

Conclusion

The incarnation means more than God's becoming man in the person of Jesus; creation itself has been transformed and witnesses to the divine presence. The Catholic sacramental imagination finds God reflected in the beauty of creation. Christian theology recognizes the divine energy sustaining all things. Even if transcendent, God is not distant. We encounter God as Father, Son, and Spirit.

Nature sings of God in the whispers of the breeze, the crashing of the surf, the music of our feathered friends. God's voice is silent, but it sounds in our inner experience, in our hearts. We should not look for "signs and wonders." They can be deceptive, lead us astray. We need to listen, to look within, and be attentive to our experience. God is subtle; his power is invitational, not controlling, or dominative.

Jesus has both a voice and a body. We hear him speak in the Gospels, and his voice is challenging. He tells us that we touch him in the poor and the needy, that he loves us and makes us his own. We meet him in his body, the church, the community of disciples. He washes away our sins, nourishes us with his body and blood, makes human love holy and life-giving, like God's. Pope Francis has struggled to make the church more welcoming, less self-absorbed. He has challenged clericalism, called on bishops to speak simply, with honesty, and to care for the wounded. He stresses that reality is more important than ideas. The Spirit moves our hearts. It endows us with gifts to serve others and to minister in Jesus's name.

In our secular society, often hostile toward religion, some psychologists and social scientists are beginning to recognize that a life of faith can contribute to our flourishing. The positive role of faith and spirituality "is often minimized or even pathologized" by mental health professionals—psychiatrists, psychologists, and nurses—as three Polish scholars acknowledge at the beginning of a well-researched article on religious values and beliefs.[22]

These scholars argue that recent research gives evidence of the helpful effects of religiosity, even for many coping with psychosis. Genuine religious practice builds hope, shapes a positive mindset, and helps bring inner peace. It can help patients recover from somatic and mental illnesses, lead to better mental health, and contribute to adolescents avoiding unhealthy behaviors, depressive symptoms, and suicide risk. While they admit that religiously based struggles can be a source of distress for some psychiatric patients, that is more often the exception than the rule. It is an indication not of healthy spirituality, but pathology.

Their research indicates that mere church membership is not enough; those who internalize their faith, who practice their beliefs and put them into practice are protected from existential anxiety and enabled to achieve a sense of their own self-value. Among the "psychological mechanisms" underlying the relationship between religious practice and mental health they list social support and social networks, which could include support from communities or church.

They also stress the need for intimacy with other persons, parents especially, important people, even God. They cite psychologists who argue that "the development of a religious, spiritual, or philosophical approach to life is one of the important indicators of human maturity. The concept of the omnipresent God provides a sense of closeness which brings a feeling of comfort, support, trust, hope, while reducing tension and anxiety in stressful and risky situations."[23]

Two researchers in the James Heft's volume *Empty Churches* came to similar conclusions: "Atheists had the highest rates of parental depression and the lowest rates of parent-child relationship closeness out of all groups, with ambivalent unreligious close behind. Highly religious had the lowest rates of parental depression and the highest rates of parent-child relationships closeness."[24]

These researchers give evidence of the positive values of a vital religious life. "Come to me, all you who labor and are burdened, and I will give you rest," says the Lord. This is an invitation that we should not refuse.

5

Jesus and Salvation

CHRISTIANITY IS A religion that promises salvation. It suggests our destiny and grounds our hope. When I ask my students what salvation means, however, most have no idea. Some will mention "going to heaven," but few are aware that salvation is something that could touch them personally, or that they themselves stand in need of it. After all, good people go to heaven when they die, as moralistic therapeutic deism, a culturally popular substitute for Christianity, presumes.[1]

Popular Christianity

Part of the problem is that popular Christianity and especially conservative evangelical Christianity have reduced the theological concept of salvation to a narrow, individualistic notion of "getting saved." If someone has been "born again" and has a "personal relationship" with Jesus, then one is home free, so to speak, with a "certainty of salvation." Justified by faith, their sins have been "covered," a legal or "forensic" concept, and they are assured of going to heaven, a gift won for us by Christ's sacrificial death on the cross, a concept that itself needs clarification.

Some evangelical theologians have acknowledged this impoverished version of the Gospel in their tradition. Scot McKnight has observed that much of evangelicalism focuses, not on Jesus and his preaching about the reign of God, but on Paul and his doctrine of justification by faith. Certainly, that has been the dominant emphasis in much of the Protestant tradition. McKnight tells us that it was only as a seminary student that he learned about Jesus and his vision of the kingdom or reign of God. Evangelicalism, he says, faces a crisis, an increasing tension "about who gets to set the terms: Jesus or Paul? In other words, will we center our Gospel teaching and living 'on the kingdom' or 'justification by faith'?"[2]

Michael Gerson makes a similar point. Raised in an evangelical home and a speech writer for George W. Bush, he writes that "Evangelicals often think that being a Christian means the individualistic acceptance of Jesus as their personal Savior. But this is quite different from following the example of Jesus we find in the Gospels. 'He never asks for admirers, worshipers or adherents....No, he calls disciples.' It is not adherents of a teaching but followers of a life Christ is looking for."[3] I have experienced this truncated version of the Gospel myself. A popular Southern Baptist leader once tried to convince me that if I couldn't point to the day and the hour that I had personally accepted Jesus, I hadn't really been saved.

The idea of salvation that we learn from the story and teaching of Jesus is both richer and deeper. To gain some insight into both, we will consider the concept of salvation in the Jewish Scriptures. Then we will look at the life of Jesus and his teaching on the reign of God. Finally, we will consider how we should understand salvation today.

Salvation in the Jewish Scriptures

The Hebrew word for salvation, *yeshu'ah*, derives from the Hebrew root *YS*, connoting open space, freedom from restraint, liberation. The archetypical Jewish understanding of salvation is the story of the exodus. The children of Israel, a Semitic people who had immigrated down to Egypt in a time of famine and were later exploited and reduced to a cruel slavery, were led out of Egypt and into the land of promise by Moses. The story, told in the Book of Exodus, is replete with various miracles worked by Moses's brother, Aaron, to convince Pharaoh to let the people go; they include a dramatic dividing of the waters of the Red Sea as they escaped from the pursuing Egyptians, God's establishing a covenant with them on Mount Sinai, and sustaining the people with miraculous nourishment during their long journey, the mysterious manna that fed them in the desert. The text speaks of "bread from heaven" and water from the rock.

Jews continue to commemorate God's saving work in the Passover meal, delivering them from slavery in Egypt and making them a people in a land of their own. With similarities to the Christian Eucharist, Passover is a ritual meal consisting of narrative and symbolic action, vegetables dipped in salty water to remind them of the tears their people shed in Egypt, matzah, the unleavened flatbread eaten in haste before the dough has had time to rise, cups of wine, and the paschal lamb, symbolizing the blood smeared on the doorposts to protect their homes from the destroying angel. Passover memorializes the saving event it commemorates; to enter it ritually is to experience its grace, rooted in their Jewish identity.

Yet the Jews continued to look forward to God's saving presence in their lives, and to future saving acts. God's promise was "I am with you" (Gen 28:15). As they moved into the Promised Land, ancient Canaan, God raised up "judges," charismatic leaders, men and women, to deliver them from their enemies. They prospered in the land, but later generations were less faithful to the Law and the covenant; they frequently fell into the idolatrous worship of their neighbors, were guilty of ignoring the needs of the poor, especially "the widows, orphans, and strangers in the land," even violating all the commandments of the Decalogue. The prophets warned the people of God's coming judgment; the northern kingdom of Israel was conquered by the Assyrians in 720 and Judah in the south fell in 587, with the people exiled to the land of the conquering Babylonians.

During these several centuries of crisis, God raised up prophets to call the people back to covenant fidelity. The prophetic preaching effected a shift in the Israelite religious imagination, away from what God had done in the past and toward a new saving action in the future (cf. Isa 43:18). Their judgment always contained a message of hope, expressed with a variety of salvific images and literary traditions.

Messianism takes its origin from Nathan's "oracle" or promise that God would raise up to David a son, an anointed or "messiah." He would be an ideal king who would deliver the people and govern righteously. God would preserve a remnant of the people. They looked forward to a Day of Yahweh when God would judge the nations and vindicate a purified Israel. He would renew his covenant or establish a new one. A Servant of the Lord would bring God's salvation to the ends of the earth and take the sins of the people upon himself, giving his life for their salvation. Thus, messianism sees salvation as a purification of national life, justice for the poor, and deliverance from enemies.

The apocalyptic tradition developed late in Jewish history. Antiochus IV (215–164), a Hellenistic king, was attempting to unite his kingdom, which included Judea, under one religion; to that end, he tried to stamp out Jewish religious faith and practice. For most of the time reflected in the Old Testament, Israelite faith included no belief in life beyond the grave, although a variant tradition in the Psalms suggests that God would not abandon the righteous to Sheol, the abode of the dead (Ps 16:9–11). When Jews under Antiochus began dying for their faith in fidelity to the covenant, however, they began looking forward to a new intervention of God, bringing the oppressive age to an end, judgment on evildoers, and raising the dead to life. Salvation meant this new intervention of God in their history, including the resurrection of the dead. Not all accepted these late developments; by the time of Jesus, the Pharisees believed in the resurrection, the more traditionalist Sadducees did not.

The very late Wisdom tradition personified divine wisdom as a feminine figure, active in creation and coming into the world with a mission (cf. Prov 1—9). The tradition continued to wrestle with the mystery of suffering, particularly of the righteous, looking to God for an answer. The Book of Job is part of this tradition. Wisdom 2 describes a just man who styles himself a child of God and calls God his father; the wicked, outraged by his righteousness, decide to put him to a shameful death to see if God will deliver him. Wisdom 3 claims that the souls of the just are in the hands of God; its body/soul binary reflects Greek influence. Wisdom theology inspired some of the New Testament writers, including both Paul and John.

These various traditions imaged Jewish hope for salvation, but what is important from a Christian perspective is that the Jewish Scriptures in all their variety are, in the final analysis, open-ended; what emerges is an expectation that Yahweh will again intervene in Israel's life, bringing a new manifestation of salvation from the God who promised to accompany his people. The images differ; some are historical, a renewal of their religious life and of the nation, reuniting Israel and Judah, even in a dramatic image bringing the dead bones of the nation to life. Others are eschatological, a new age of justice and peace, a restoration of paradise when even the animals are at peace with one another, and Jerusalem would be a light for all the nations.[4] Still others look forward to the resurrection of the dead.

Jesus and the Kingdom/ Reign of God

The image that dominated Jesus's preaching was the kingdom of God, a metaphor or symbol for salvific grace at the very center of his ministry. The kingdom of God—or better, *reign* of God—was not a place but a dynamic activity; it means God's power, God's grace, God's salvation breaking into the world and into our lives in a new way. For the sake of familiarity, I will use both terms here. The reign of God is neither simply present nor simply future; it is both.

As a symbol, it is polyvalent; as Eamon Bredin notes, it is "approaching," "coming," "at hand." Jesus calls others to "enter into" or "seek" it. Some are "not far" from it, while others fail to enter it. The mystery of the kingdom is not revealed to everyone, but only to the disciples. The keys to the kingdom are given to Simon Peter. Most of all the kingdom "has come upon you" or "is in the midst of you."[5]

In a marvelous phrase, Elizabeth Johnson describes Jesus as not just speaking about the kingdom, but "enacting" it in his ministry.[6] His preaching and parables show others that the reign of God was already at hand. In healing the sick and driving out evil or oppressive spirits, he was bringing God's saving grace into their bodies and healing their own spirits. Those who had been estranged from their communities by illness or possession were freed from their isolation, liberated, and returned to families and society. In reaching out to sinners and proclaiming forgiveness of their sins, he was enabling them also to experience God's salvation.

Jesus also enacted God's reign in his table fellowship. Meals played an important role in his ministry. The Gospels show him frequently sharing meals with others, with the multitude that followed him, feeding them miraculously, with his disciples, with some of the Pharisees and Scribes who opposed him, and with sinners, a practice that occasioned considerable criticism. There was an inclusive character to his meals. In one of my favorite passages, in a moment of frustration Jesus rebukes his critics who listened neither to John the Baptist nor to himself, insulting them both:

> To what shall I compare this generation? It is like children who sit in marketplaces and call to one another, "We played the flute for you, but you did not dance, we sang a dirge but you did not mourn." For John came neither

eating nor drinking, and they said, "He is possessed by a demon." The Son of Man came eating and drinking and they said, "Look, he is a glutton and a drunkard, a friend of tax collectors and sinners." (Matt 11:17–19)

The table fellowship tradition shows Jesus reaching out to others, especially to sinners, to those who needed him most, welcoming them, assuring them of God's mercy, showing them that no one was excluded from God's reign. In more intimate gatherings he taught his own. In all this, he was bringing God's saving grace into peoples' lives.

It is also important to stress that in Jesus's ministry the kingdom of God was not yet present in its fullness. In the Lord's prayer he taught his disciples to pray, "Thy kingdom come." The sayings about the Son of Man coming in judgment reflect the future dimension of the kingdom (cf. Mark 14:62; Matt 25:31–32; 26:64; Luke 12:8–9). The parables of the kingdom in Matthew 13—the sower and the seed, the weeds and the wheat, the mustard seed, the yeast kneaded in the flour, the net cast into the sea—show both its present and future dimensions. This dual realization of the reign is also present in John's Gospel, although John substitutes "eternal life" for the reign of God. Here, Jesus says, "Those who eat my flesh and drink my blood have eternal life, and I will raise them up on the last day" (6:54). It is only in the resurrection of Jesus that we gain an insight into the full realization of the reign of God, the fullness of God's salvation. These dual dimensions of the kingdom or reign of God are present also in Vatican II's *Dogmatic Constitution on the Church* (cf. LG 5).

Jesus's death on the cross is often seen as the price paid for our salvation, based on Anselm's concept of substitutionary atonement in his book, *Cur Deus Homo?* (Why Did God Become Man?). An eleventh-century monk and archbishop of Canterbury, Anselm argued that only an infinite victim could compensate for the offense against an infinite God and restore the order of creation, damaged by Adam's sin. Thus, God became human to save us from our sins. Even the present Catholic liturgical translation reflects this view.

This is problematic on several grounds, however. It makes human sinfulness the reason for the incarnation, rather than recognizing the role of the Word in creation, itself God's saving work. Salvation becomes dependent on the death of Jesus, rather than on his entire life, ministry, proclamation of the kingdom, and his resurrection. Pastorally, it seems to demand the sacrifice of God's only begotten Son, obscuring God's love and mercy, an emphasis that has done considerable damage to Christian preaching and spirituality and remains an obstacle to faith. Jesus died because he was faithful to his ministry, despite the opposition it aroused. This was the price that Jesus paid, not because his death was a necessary offering to save us from our sins. The New Testament's language of redemption and atonement is metaphorical.

The early Christians believed that God's salvation had been revealed in Jesus's preaching, in his resurrection from the dead and gift of the Spirit. Just as it did for the prophets of old, God's salvation included justice for the poor and creation itself, looking forward to a new heaven and a new earth (cf. Rev 21:1; 2 Pet 3:13), to be considered later. When the early Christians gathered for Eucharist, they prayed, "Come Lord Jesus, generally facing towards the East in their celebrations to meet Jesus when like the rising sun he would come in glory."

The Eastern and Western churches approached salvation differently. "Why did God become human? 'To save us,' says the West. 'So that the human being may become God,' affirms the East. These two expressions are complementary: God became human, so that humanity could become truly human, as he intended and created him to be; humanity, whose icon is the Son."[7]

TO BELIEVE OR NOT BELIEVE

Understanding the Kingdom Today

If the kingdom of God was initially present in Jesus's ministry, so should it be present today. Vatican II speaks of Christ as having "inaugurated the Kingdom of heaven on earth and revealed to us the mystery of that kingdom. By His obedience He brought about redemption. The Church, or, in other words, the kingdom of Christ now present in mystery, grows visibly through the power of God in the world" (LG 3), but the symbolic language of Scripture and church always need to be translated anew.

Jesus's ministry had a strong social dimension. If he called the poor blessed, restored the broken and the banished to society, praised peacemakers, and welcomed all, always trying to bring people together; if he proclaimed good news to the poor, liberty to captives, and sent his disciples forth to drive out oppressive spirits, we can at least say where the kingdom or God's reign is absent. It is not present where dishonesty prevails, human rights are not respected, or human life not valued. It is absent where self-interest is placed ahead of the common good, polarizing communities rather than striving for unity and communion. It is not present where people are victims of injustice, where there is exploitation by others, or where people suffer violence. It is gone where racist attitudes or structures disadvantage people of color or deny them opportunity. When the nation of South Africa still lived under the policy of "apartheid," separating people because of race even at the eucharistic table, both the Lutheran World Federation and the World Alliance of Reformed Churches (now World Communion) broke communion with their South African member churches. They saw their support for apartheid as radically contrary to the Gospel.

From early in his academic career, Joseph Ratzinger cautioned against any attempt to "immanentize" the eschaton, reducing it to an earthly, political reality rather than a transcendent one, to make it something in history rather than beyond it. This was the mistake of Karl Marx, as Pope Benedict argued in his encyclical *Spe Salvi* (no.

20), but that does not in any way take away from the social dimensions of Jesus's preaching. Ratzinger/Pope Benedict addressed some of these themes in his 2009 encyclical *Caritas in Veritate*.

As Roger Haight writes, "Christian revelation reveals human existence as standing before the face of God."[8] But God's otherness or holiness is blinding, revealing our own sinfulness. If God is holy, we should be holy also. Thus, there is an ethical dimension to standing before God who is the fullness of truth, goodness, and beauty. To stand in this relationship is to be in what the Christian tradition has called the state of grace, but grace is not a thing, something that increases or diminishes within us, like milk in a milk bottle (as Sister used to say in school, in those days when we still had milk bottles).

Grace, from the Greek *charis*, for loving kindness or favor, is a relationship between each of us and God, but it is even more than a relationship; it is to share in God's life. As Karl Rahner notes, grace is God's free self-communication, for we human beings are not just open to the infinite but drawn to what we already intuit or grasp "non-thematically." "*Self*-communication of the absolutely *holy* God designates a quality sanctifying man prior to his free and good decision."[9]

To live in righteousness and justice, to help others flourish, to be peacemakers and reconcilers, to bring good news to the poor, comfort to the afflicted, to bring people together and build community is to live in God's transforming grace. Or as Pope Francis says, in different words but with the same meaning: "The human person grows more, matures more and is sanctified more to the extent that he or she enters into relationships, going out from themselves to live in communion with God, with others and with all creatures. In this way, they make their own that trinitarian dynamism which God imprinted in them when they were created."[10] But in our freedom, we can also turn from this relationship, this self-communication of the divine. The Christian tradition calls turning away from God's presence sin.

Jesus's metaphor of the kingdom or reign of God tells us that the transcendent God is not distant from us. In the language of the

New Testament, the reign of God is approaching, near, in our midst; it means God dwelling within us, God's Spirit guiding us. In more contemporary language, the reign is a symbol for God's presence, love, and grace, a grace that heals wounds and liberates others from unjust systems and practices. Terrence Tilley says the reign of God is a realm of human flourishing. As Christians, we witness to this reign, as did those in the Jesus movement, by healing, exorcising, sharing table fellowship, forgiving, and teaching, not just in regard to individuals but by working to transform society.[11]

Schillebeeckx notes that God's grace is mediated by human beings caring for one another.[12] Or according to Albert Nolan, it is precisely human compassion that "releases God's power in the world, the only power that can bring about the miracle of the kingdom."[13] Perhaps St. Paul expressed this best when he wrote, "The kingdom of God is not a matter of food and drink, but of righteousness, peace, and joy in the Holy Spirit" (Rom 14:17).

But the fullness of the reign of God, God's salvation, revealed in the resurrection of Jesus, also embraces us. The joyful proclamation that God raised Jesus from the dead stands at the very center of the New Testament. It gathered the disciples who had fled Jerusalem at Jesus's arrest, to await the outpouring of the Spirit; they began their witnessing, preaching, writing, and the church itself. Jesus's resurrection is also ours; his glory is our ultimate hope. St. Paul addresses all of us when he says so beautifully, "Awake, O sleeper, and rise from the dead, and Christ will give you light" (Eph 5:14). In the iconography of the Orthodox churches, Jesus never raises alone, but always in company with others. In the Apostles' Creed, we say, "He descended into hell," meaning not just that Jesus truly died, but that he descended to the realm of the dead, bringing them hope.[14]

In his beautiful 2007 encyclical *Spe Salvi*, in English "Saved in Hope," Pope Benedict XVI criticized the modern, individualistic understanding of salvation so widespread today, seeing it as a private form of salvation. Instead, he speaks of salvation as a social reality. Redemption means a restoration of unity, undoing the fragmentation and division symbolized by the biblical story of the Tower of Babel. It begins now, in the communion of persons that is the church, works to bring about greater unity in this world as it looks forward to its fullness in the world to come.

Thus, it begins with a people. It happens only in this "we," liberating us from the prison of our individual "I." God's grace is unifying, not divisive (SS 13–15). Benedict's vision is powerful, one that speaks to us in our polarized social, political, even ecclesial lives. We see elected representatives shouting and abusing each other in Congress; our society is divided by issues of economic status, white supremacy, antisemitism, prejudice against those who are sexually and culturally different; we are scandalized when, even in the Church, our bishops are divided, conservatives and liberals, culture warriors and progressives, bishops who were once ultramontane now openly criticizing Pope Francis. We need God's salvific grace.

God's salvation is even more. The resurrection of Jesus affects not just us but all creation. As Walter Kasper once wrote, through "Jesus' Resurrection and Exaltation a 'piece of this world' finally reached God and was finally accepted by God."[15] This is also the vision of Elizabeth Johnson; she says that the symbol of the reign of God "evokes the final age when the Spirit will be poured out, when creation will be made whole…when God's will is finally done on earth as it is in heaven and the well-being and salvation of every human person and of all creation is secured."[16] We see this in Catholic evolutionary thinkers like Johnson, John Haught, and Ilia Delio who see God as continuing to work through the evolutionary process, drawing all creation to its ultimate fulfillment in Christ, a vision that is fundamentally Pauline. We need to consider this more carefully.

Indeterminacy and Evolution

So, how might we imagine God's ongoing creative work? The universe has its own laws, imperfect as they are, but they are not absolute. One of the implications of quantum mechanics is that indeterminacy lurks at the very heart of things. Focused on the world of subatomic particles, Heisenberg's uncertainty principle asserts that certain complementary values such as momentum and position can be predicted only within certain limits. The more precisely the position of a particle is determined, the less precisely can its momentum be assessed, and vice versa. Einstein disagreed; he countered that this apparent indeterminacy or randomness was only a reflection of our ignorance. He once said famously, "God does not play dice."

For some thinkers, the process philosophers among them, quantum mechanics suggests that, at its most fundamental level, reality exhibits an uncertainty or "indeterminacy" (*Ungenauigkeit*, the German term that Heisenberg first used in 1927). If this is so, then reality is not a mechanism, a philosophical view held by Laplace (1749–1827) and others that saw the universe as reducible to mechanical principles. They theorized that if it were possible to know the mass and motion of all microscopic particles, one could accurately predict the future. To the contrary, quantum physics shows an indeterminacy or spontaneity at the heart of nature, an ontological ground for choice that one day, given an evolutionary perspective, might develop into spontaneity and freedom. As we saw earlier, our beautiful world remains unfinished. God is still at work.

Elizabeth Johnson describes God from an evolutionary perspective. God does not intervene in the world to accomplish the divine purpose but works in and through natural causes, including those chance events that allow novelty to emerge. "At every moment divine agency will be physically undetectable. It is not a quantifiable property like mass or energy, not an additional factor in the equations, not an element that can be discovered among the forces of the universe at all. But in and through the creativity of nature, the boundless love of the creator Spirit is bringing the world to birth."[17] Theologically, such a view is far from seeing God as a cosmic monarch, exercising an absolute control, and it suggests that we need to rethink the traditional view of God's omnipotence.

We do not always recognize the Spirit's work. Someone once asked Cardinal Joseph Ratzinger if it was the Holy Spirit that chose the pope when the cardinals gathered in conclave. He cautiously replied, "I would say that the Spirit does not exactly take control of the affair, but rather like a good educator, as it were, leaves us much space, much freedom, without entirely abandoning us....There are too many contrary instances of popes the Holy Spirit would obviously not have picked."[18]

Rethinking God's omnipotence takes nothing away from the divine agency. We confess God as creator, bringing the vast universe into being out of nothing and sustaining it in his loving care. Creation was not something that occurred once and for all in the past, but is ongoing, a continuous creation (*creatio continua*). As the psalmist sings, "You raise grass for the cattle and plants for our beasts of burden. You bring bread from the earth and wine to gladden our hearts" (Ps 104:14). Yet if God intended to create a world in which his children could respond in love, it had to be a world rooted in a spontaneity that could one day develop into freedom, implying a self-limitation of the divine power. Pope John Paul II once wrote, "In a certain sense one could say that *confronted with our human freedom God decided to make himself 'impotent'*."[19]

God's work is not finished. St. Ignatius of Loyola says in his *Spiritual Exercises* that God "works and labors for me in all creatures upon the face of the earth" (no. 236). Evolutionary thinkers like Johnson, John Haught, and Ilia Delio, influenced by the Jesuit paleontologist and visionary Teilhard de Chardin, see God working in and through creation to bring it to fulfillment. Haught sees evolution as described by Darwin as a drama, with each living species struggling to be and to flourish, a risky struggle with considerable loss and failure in the story.[20] He describes a hidden God who draws the cosmos forward, citing Karl Rahner, who sees God as the world's "Absolute Future."[21] This is what evolutionary materialists cannot see; they reduce the story of life to a series of accidents, pure chance, mindless physical components without subjectivity and spirit. Like

Teilhard, Ilia Delio, a Franciscan sister, sees Christ at the heart of the evolutionary process, bringing about unity "in the divine, continual act of creation, redemption, and sanctification of the total universe."[22] Her view is rooted in Scripture, which sees Christ's creative work as ongoing. This view is biblical.

Paul describes creation as groaning in labor pains, hoping to be set free from corruption and share in the glorious freedom of the children of God (cf. Rom 8:21–22); "all things were created through him and for him. He is before all things, and in him all things hold together" (Col 1:16–17). Christ will reign until he has put all his enemies under his feet, and then when everything has been subjected to him, he will be subjected to God, so that God may be all in all (cf. 1 Cor 15:25–28). The visionary author of the Book of Revelation looks forward to "a new heaven and a new earth" (Rev 21:1; cf. 2 Pet 3:13), describing Christ as the Alpha and the Omega, the first and the last, the beginning and the end (Rev 22:13). In a real sense, creation and eschatology are corelative concepts.

Scripture also speaks of Jesus, who "emptied himself," giving up equality with God, taking the form of a slave (Phil 2:6–11). This leads to another image or model of God, a *kenotic model*, which sees a nondominative God who creates not by using power but by "letting-be, by making room, and by withdrawing himself."[23] Such a God cannot intervene to "fix" those tragedies or evils that so often occur. The world has its own causality. Or in the words of John Haught, this is a God whose "unobtrusive and self-absenting mode of being invites the world to swell forth continually through immense epochs of temporal duration and experimentation, into an always free and open future, and to do so in the relatively autonomous mode of 'self-creation' that science has discerned in cosmic, biological, and cultural evolution."[24]

This does not mean a God without power, but a God whose power is invitational, not dominative. This is a God who chooses to reject all violence or coercion, all signs of the demonic, a God who calls and inspires and becomes vulnerable, as Jesus was, even a God who suffers. Edward Schillebeeckx says, "By creating human beings with their own finite and free will, God voluntarily renounces power."[25] The American philosopher Alfred North Whitehead in reflecting on God's engagement with the human described him as "the fellow sufferer who understands."[26] Pope John Paul said something similar in his 1998 encyclical *Fides et Ratio*. From the perspective of the passion of Jesus, "the prime commitment of theology is seen to be the understanding of God's *kenosis*, a grand and mysterious truth for the human mind, which finds it inconceivable that suffering and death can express a love which gives itself and seeks nothing in return" (no. 93). Our language here, of course, like all theological language, is metaphorical; still, it expresses a truth that comes not from reason alone but from biblical revelation.

Christology

The understanding of Jesus that comes from the New Testament and the doctrine of the later Church expressed in its creeds took a while to emerge, although one finds some high Christology early in the New Testament, contrary to what was commonly alleged in an earlier theological liberalism. Critical scholarship has recovered certain elements from the actual words and deeds of the Jesus of history, which suggest that he had some sense of his unique authority and relation to the God of Israel, most probably an intuition rather than a conceptual awareness, although our knowledge here is limited. We have little access to Jesus's self-understanding, but there are clues.

First, as we have seen, Jesus addressed God as Abba, using an intimate, familial term for one's father that no Jew of the time would have dared to use in speaking to or about God. Second, the sources suggest that Jesus, in interpreting the place of the law in Jewish life, sometimes placed his authority above that of the lawgiver, Moses. The late John P. Meier, in his massive investigation of the historical

Jesus, points to Jesus's saying on Sabbath observance (cf. Mark 2:27) and his seeming indifference to laws about ritual purity. He argues that the double command to love God and neighbor as well as the command to love one's enemies very likely go back to the historical Jesus.[27] There is here an implicit claim to authority.

The earliest New Testament documents are the authentic letters of Paul, appearing almost twenty years before the first Gospel. They give several examples of a very early high Christology, a theology aware of Jesus's divine status as early as Paul or even earlier. They include the title *Kyrios* or Lord, the fact that for the early Christian communities Jesus was an object of worship, and hymns or passages celebrating his divine status, what theologians call a preexistence theology.[28]

While Jesus may have been recognized as messiah even during his lifetime (cf. Mark 8:29), the early Christians communities addressed Jesus as "Lord," using both the Greek *kyrios* and Aramaic *mar*. Although *kyrios* was at time a polite form of address, like "master" or sir," it was also used in addressing the gods or God. Yet what is significant for the earliest Jewish Christians is that *kyrios* was used in the Septuagint, the Greek translation of the Jewish Scriptures, to translate the holy name of Yahweh. In other words, it was a divine title.

We know also that Aramaic-speaking communities addressed Jesus as *mar* while Greek-speaking Christians used *kyrios*. Paul gives evidence of both usages. He sometimes used *kyrios* in referring to God, but most often he uses it as a title for Jesus, some 180 times. His most common term for Jesus was Lord Jesus Christ. He cites the Aramaic invocation *Marana tha* ("Our Lord come") for his Greek-speaking congregations without translating it (1 Cor 16:22).

Larry Hurtado argues that Jesus was worshipped in early Christianity. He points to a "binitarian" pattern of devotion, song, and invocation, sometimes invoking God and Jesus together (cf. Rom 16:20), baptizing others in his name, and celebrating his redemptive death in the Eucharist, not as a dead hero but as a living and reigning Lord.

Jesus and Salvation

Some early hymns or confessions cited by Paul are also evidence for early preexistence Christology. We see it in the famous Philippian hymn (Phil 2:6–11), a pre-Pauline Christian hymn taken up by Paul to acclaim Jesus as one "Who, though he was in the form of God did not regard equality with God something to be grasped. Rather he emptied himself, taking the form of a slave, coming in human likeness, and found human in appearance." A similar text occurs in 2 Corinthians 8:9. Another speaks of "one Lord, Jesus Christ, through whom all things are and through whom we exist" (1 Cor 8:6), recognizing his role in creation. We've spent some time on Paul's authentic letters to show that recognition of Jesus's preexistence and role in creation is not some late development, still less a "Hellenization" of the church's faith as often claimed by theological liberalism, but very early.

The canonical Gospels show further evidence of the christological development. Mark, the first Gospel written about the year 70, portrays Jesus as Messiah and suffering Son of Man, but his root metaphor is Son of God, in a sense more functional, than ontological. Yet there are moments when Mark suggests that Jesus is something more. In telling the story of Jesus coming to his disciples in the boat, walking on the waters, he says paradoxically, "He meant to pass by them" (Mark 6:48). This echoes a similar passage in Job where God treads on the sea and passes by (Job 9:8,11). The similarty is not accidental.

Matthew and Luke's Gospels were written in the mid-80s. Matthew portrays Jesus as the new Moses who teaches with authority, three times referring to himself as "the Son." Like Luke, he includes testimony to Jesus's virginal conception, suggesting his unique sonship. Luke does not show the disciples referring to Jesus as Son of God during his ministry. He seems to see Jesus as God's representative on earth, empowered with the Spirit, but John's Gospel, written around 95, represents the most developed Christology in the New Testament. The prologue, another early Christian hymn, echoes the Old Testament Wisdom theology, though substituting Word for

Wisdom. It shows Jesus as Word, active in creation, becoming flesh as God's only Son. Jesus speaks openly of his union with the father and says that he has come down from heaven (John 6:38). He frequently uses the divine formula, "I AM" (*egō eimi*). At the end of the Gospel, when the doubting Thomas probes the risen Jesus's wounds, he exclaims, "My Lord and My God," one of the few times that *Theos* (God) is predicated of Jesus (John 20:28; cf. John 1:1; Heb 1:8–9).

Conclusion

Jürgen Moltmann, a German prisoner of war who became a Christian after someone gave him a copy of the New Testament, once said, "If Christian hope is reduced to the salvation of the soul in a heaven beyond death, it loses its power to renew life and change the world, and its flame is quenched."[29] In this chapter, we have tried to set forth a deeper concept of salvation. Running through it have been three interconnected themes: the kingdom or reign of God, grace, and salvation.

The kingdom of God was the metaphor or symbol at the center of Jesus's preaching. Building on the invocation of God as king, over Israel, over the nations, and over all creation in the Jewish Scriptures, Jesus rephrased it as the kingdom or reign of God. For him it meant God's presence or power, evident in his healings, exorcisms, and proclamation of the forgiveness of sins, while the fullness of God's reign is revealed in his resurrection.

Grace refers to God's free self-communication, sensed intuitively while remaining mystery. Grace and the Spirit are virtually synonymous. Salvation refers to God's grace or Spirit transforming us in this life and fully in the life to come. The Incarnation suggests God's solidarity not only with the just but with all creation.

Today, many young Christians seem to have little idea of what salvation means or why they might stand in need of it. The biblical concept of salvation is both richer and deeper than the "I got saved" version of conservative Christianity. Israel's enduring paradigm for salvation is the exodus story, God's deliverance of the children of Israel from slavery in Egypt and making them his people. Liberation is another way of speaking about salvation, liberation from sin, from estrangement, from a life without hope.

The Old Testament ends with a sense of expectation; Israel stands in need for God's coming in a new way. Christians see this realized in the story of Jesus. Known to us mainly from the canonical Gospels, but also from a few nonbiblical sources, Jesus in his ministry proclaimed the nearness of the reign of God, his polyvalent symbol for God's saving grace or presence. It was already present in his ministry, and he taught his disciples to pray for its coming in its fullness.

The kingdom or reign of God needs to be translated anew for every age. The gift of grace is gratuitous, but we must freely accept it. It unites us to Christ, transforms us, and gives us a share in God's life. To live in God's presence calls us to be righteous and holy. God's saving grace, ours in Christ Jesus, is mediated by men and women caring for one another. It challenges us to bring the good news of salvation to others, to comfort the afflicted, work for justice, and care for creation. As Pope Francis says in his encyclical *Laudato Si'*, we need to hear both the cry of the earth and the cry of the poor (no. 49).

The resurrection of Jesus reveals the fullness of the kingdom, foreshadowing the day when creation itself will share in a salvation that is cosmic as well as personal.[30] We need to take the trinitarian and communal dimensions of salvation seriously; salvation is fundamentally a corporate concept. We celebrate God's presence among us in the community of the church and encounter Christ in its Scriptures and sacraments.

Although a credal formulation of the mystery of Jesus the Christ took several centuries to develop, the Church's confession of faith is rooted in the words and deeds of the Jesus of history and is already evident in some of the earliest New Testament documents. If we are unable to show that the Church's christological faith is rooted in the person of Jesus himself, it remains open to the charge of some that the Church Hellenized or divinized Jesus in its theology. The creed safeguards our trinitarian faith and our belief in the resurrection of the dead.

Some theologians continue to believe that in the mystery of God's providence all will be saved. David Bentley Hart appeals to certain church fathers in the first five centuries, among them Origen, Gregory of Nyssa, Isaac of Nineveh, and Maximus the Confessor, who held for universal salvation (*apokatatasis*). Hart argues that a God who creates the world in which eternal torment was possible for some, even if it were the result of their own free choice, would not be the infinitively good God of Christianity. He says that the punishing God in whom most Christians have believed appears as evil; he rejects as illogical the arguments of those he dismisses somewhat ungraciously as "infernalists."[31]

As I get older, I gain a deeper sense of my own need for God's salvation. I am more conscious of my own sinfulness. I try to live justly, but so often fall short. I long for God's transforming grace. The world itself is hurting. There is so much injustice, so much needless suffering, so many innocent victims. Many continue to question the goodness of God and ask, does God really care? I find myself asking, does God really hear the cries of the poor? But the story of Jesus gives us hope. It assures us that evil does not have the last word.

Epilogue

FAITH REMAINS A gift, something we must be open to receiving. In today's world, with a culture often hostile to faith and with so much suffering and injustice, so many distractions, and truth itself often difficult to find, it's not easy to be a believer. Nor can we make another believe with arguments. Faith is not a collection of doctrines. As Pope Francis insists, it's about a relationship, a person, Jesus.[1] It is Jesus who enables us to see and gladdens our hearts. In closing, I offer some concluding reflections, summarizing some of what we have considered and offering a few suggestions.

    1. The loss of teenagers and young adults, not just from their churches but often from the faith itself, is a concern to all our churches and religious communities. While Catholic losses are less than those of the mainline Protestant, they are still significant. Lapsed Catholics, some 20 million, could be considered the second largest religious denomination in the United States, surpassed only by practicing Catholics. Some young Catholics are described as "liminal nones," halfway between being religious and secular in their identities; some of them continuing Catholic practices such as prayer, occasional worship, or sending their children to Catholic schools. The good news is that many of our young people still have Christian values, but are impatient with a church they perceive as concerned only with rules and doctrines.

TO BELIEVE OR NOT BELIEVE

In the United States today, with its growing Hispanic population, 30 percent of Hispanic Catholics are disaffiliated, up from 10 percent in 2010, including half of those who are under the age of thirty. Hispanic Catholics make up 62 percent of Catholics under the age of eighteen. The percentage of Latino Protestants has remained relatively stable, though evangelical Latino congregations are growing, and Latino evangelicals appear more involved with their faith than Catholics.[2] All our churches need the energy and giftedness of these young adults. Without them, the church has no future. They are not all indifferent to questions of faith and many of them sense that something is missing in their lives. They are looking for something that gives their lives meaning.[3] The explanations for disaffiliation are numerous, but several stand out. Many are the children of nonpracticing parents. Most researchers see parental practice as the most important factor in passing on the faith to the young. The commitment of fathers is especially important. The culture in which young adults are raised is decidedly secular and individualistic. It has reduced religion to the private and the subjective.

According to the CARA report on the spiritual life of Catholics, the church's outreach to young adults during the pandemic was minimal; only 18 percent were contacted by their parishes among those registered, those unregistered far less.[4] Nor are Catholic parishes always as welcoming to Hispanics as evangelical communities, which often proselytize them and offer them more opportunities for leadership. Hispanic children are also underrepresented in Catholic schools. They often find their priests rigid, negative in their preaching, and stressing rules. Father Greg Boyle says that when he first began to preach at Dolores Mission, a parish in the midst of three housing projects, the people leaving church would ask him to "chew them out," telling them how they failed to measure up to God's high expectations. This is what they had come to expect from their priests.[5]

2. Many young Catholics are virtually illiterate when it comes to Christian faith. They know little about the Catholic tradition, but they also find their churches too judgmental, often at odds with their

own values, intolerant of those who are different, especially those in the LGBTQ community. Other concerns include racism and the environment. Young evangelicals are also diminishing, as many white evangelicals seem to identify being a Christian with identifying with the extreme right-wing of the Republican party whose values are opposites to their own.[6]

3. Social scientists have also pointed to widespread social dislocation today and the loss of a sense of community. Along with religious disaffiliation, they chart a growing loss of trust in one's neighbors and a diminished involvement in civic and philanthropic engagement, while self-help groups continue to multiply. Despite numerous virtual friends on digital platforms, many young people have few real friends. An increasing number of them report feelings of sadness and loneliness, especially for those who are heavy users of social media. They find the use of alcohol and suicide attempts rising, especially among girls.

4. So how should pastoral ministers try to reach these young people? Starting with theology and the church's official doctrine is not the best approach. They need more than the *Catechism of the Catholic Church*. They want something more personal and welcoming, a church able to meet them where they are, one that listens rather than simply instructs. The CARA survey "Faith and Spiritual Life of Catholics in the United States" (2021) reported "a perceived general reluctance to actually *listen* to youth and young adults and grant them true *agency* in the ecclesial community."[7]

The *Instrumentum Laboris* for the synod on synodality recognizes young people "as subjects and not objects of pastoral care" (B 2.1) and asks how to foster their participation with other marginalized voices "in discernment and decision-making (B 3.2).[8] Pope Francis sees the very meaning of synodality as walking together as the People of God. Do our pastoral ministers walk together with our young adults? At the 2023 Synod on Synodality in Rome, the participants included lay men and women in their twenties and thirties as well as some college students, all with voting rights, gathered with the bishops, not in hierarchical order but at round tables where they could talk with each other. Cardinal Jean-Claude Hollerich, the papal appointed "relator" or moderator of the synod instructed them that their reflections "should not take the form of a theological or sociological treatise," but should start "from concrete experiences, our own personal one and above all the collective experience of the people of God."[9] So the voices of some young people were heard at the synod. A picture of the participants at their round tables said it all.

    5. Church ministers need to discover the concerns of young adults. In addition to dealing with loneliness, depression, and a certain lack of hope, many are concerned with more existential issues; why not begin with these? These are issues that touch them where they live. They also need to be able to raise difficult questions where they disagree with church teaching. What helps are supportive communities where they can share their struggles with faith, learn from each other, and discover a more personal God, beyond the vague "higher power," to which so many refer.

    Christian Smith finds two things most important. First, young adults need models, mentors, teachers, and friends serious about their faith. They need companions and accompaniment. Second is the commitment and example of Catholic parents. While their children will make their own decisions, the good example of their parents is often what makes the difference.[10]

    New pastoral initiatives can also be helpful. John Paul II established World Youth Day in 1985 to bring young Catholics together from around the world to celebrate their faith and culture together with the pope. They come by the thousands, as they do to the ecumenical community of Taizé in France to join in the prayer, song, and silence in a church lit by candles. Pope Francis has made it possible for some young adults to participate in the synod on synodality in Rome, mentioned earlier.

    More than two hundred Catholic parishes, mostly in the United States, have LGBTQ ministries, and the number continues

Epilogue

to grow. Other efforts include Theology on Tap, young adult groups, and *Pastoral Juvenil Hispana* groups, often including recent migrants. Outreach to young Hispanics, already the majority among young Catholics, is especially important.[11] The Archdiocese of Seattle has set up a new program as part of the synod process to reach out to a hundred people baptized but no longer practicing. The Archdiocese of Baltimore has found a new policy of allowing Catholic couples to celebrate their marriages outside a church to be highly successful. The chancellor of the archdiocese said that the policy has been greeted with enthusiasm by many priests and married couples. Personal invitations to join a church community from friends, peers especially, are most effective.

6. The dominance of social media today is another problem. Some 95 percent of teens in the United States use digital devices, spending an average of two to three hours a day online, often considerably more, but increasing evidence points to the negative influence of these platforms, including diminished social skills, limited attention spans, addiction, and loss of sleep. More serious problems include online bullying and sexual trafficking as well as media platforms using artificial intelligence to reinforce their users' interests, rather than broadening their perspectives.

With easy access to social media, anyone regardless of educational credentials can be "published," allowing individuals and politicians to spread personal views, disinformation, and conspiracy theories, while hostile foreign agents use the internet to engage in cyber warfare. As more and more people get their information from social media rather than newspapers, reputable news sources, and scholarly journals, the general population is becoming increasingly illiterate. Vicious attacks on political opponents that one sees constantly on Instagram are symptomatic of a society that no longer values civility and truth.

The fascination with digital images and videos suggests the need for a new approach to mental health, an asceticism that limits time spent on social media platforms, a revival of the ancient spiritual discipline of fasting, not from food but from the constant stimulation of their digital screens. Young people also need times of interior silence. As gyms and sport clubs multiply across the land, a great deal of time and expense is spent on caring for the body. But what about caring for the soul? Too often that is ignored.

7. The Catholic Church could use social media with greater effectiveness. Bishop Robert Barron is one example of someone who makes good use of today's digital culture for evangelization. Recent posts are apologetic, arguing the historical roots of Catholicism and the authenticity of its tradition. Increasingly, they address serious theological questions. Some religious communities showcase their lives with online pictures of attractive monastics and beautiful liturgies, but, as Hosffman Ospino says, "Many—most?—Catholic pastoral leaders seem to be oblivious about using social media to engage their constituencies, especially the young."[12] Pastoral leaders could engage young adults, more familiar with today's digital culture, to be of assistance here.

Unfortunately, Catholic media is too often dominated by traditionalists and the right wing. Mother Angelica's EWTN, which is openly hostile to Pope Francis, is just one example. There are frequent online postings of very traditional religious communities with elaborate videos of Tridentine liturgies, with priests facing the wall in fiddleback vestments and maniples. This in no way reflects contemporary Catholicism.

8. Modernity's focus on the subject has also contributed to a loss of transcendence. All too often, a crude scientism has resulted in a constricted theory of knowledge and metaphysical skepticism. Lost is any sense of the spiritual dimension of the human, while personal tragedies and widespread suffering result in a tendency to blame the Creator or reject belief in his existence. The culture of modernity and social media have both contributed to the "dictatorship of relativism" that Cardinal Ratzinger spoke of shortly before his election to the Chair of Peter. We need to recover an epistemology mindful of the spiritual dimension of human knowing, its ability

to transcend the material and recognize the transcendent to which it is ordered.

9. The idea of a humanistic education is disappearing as universities, sensitive to student and parent employment concerns, reduce programs in the humanities in favor of business and career-oriented courses. Teaching critical thinking is especially important, especially with so many dependent on social media and so much disinformation. Students need to learn how to discern truth from mere rhetoric. This makes the tradition of a liberal arts education so much more important, though difficult, with so little financial support for education, public or private.

Many students today seem more fragile. Political correctness has been broadened considerably to a concern for "emotional well-being." Students demand to have their "comfort" animals on campus. They want "safe spaces" and "trigger warnings" to mark ideas or narratives that might be challenging or cause "emotional distress," and punishment for those deemed guilty of speech considered offensive. Will students examine only those ideas with which they feel comfortable?

10. The Catholic Church has a wide network of colleges and universities, more than two hundred in the United States serving more than 870,000 students, but many of them are becoming increasingly distant from the Catholic tradition. Some have already dropped majors in philosophy and theology.[13] While they may have campus ministries and departments of theology or religious studies, Catholic faculty members are usually in the minority, often as low as 30 percent. Their colleagues are not always open to the Catholic tradition; some actively oppose it. What this means is that there are few living bearers of the tradition who might be examples to Catholic students, struggling to find their own way to a mature faith. They need to learn that one can be a faithful Catholic and still respectfully disagree with some church teachings.

Massimo Faggioli has often pointed to the estrangement between academic theology and the institutional Church, suggesting that this is one reason many younger Catholics are now turning to neo-traditionalist circles for instruction.[14] Some neo-conservative Catholic institutions seem to hire and serve only Catholics. With approximately 98 percent Catholic professors and students, how do these schools enter effectively into a dialogue with culture? Are they only saving the saved?

The current emphasis on diversity, equity, and inclusion (DEI) has exacerbated the situation; faculty members and administrators continue to emphasize DEI in hiring processes with departmental and college DEI representatives to make sure it is stressed. However, rarely is attention given to the institution's Catholic mission and the need for Catholic representatives of the tradition among its faculty. As a positive example, Catholic faculty members at Yale have been invited to speak after the student Masses, not about their scholarship and research but their personal faith.

11. A common attitude today sees religion and science as antithetical, but faith and reason are different ways of knowing and should work in harmony. From early in Christian history, scholars and theologians have been willing to learn from secular wisdom, though as we saw earlier, history has witnessed some embarrassing exceptions. Still, the Church's evangelical mission encourages it to find culturally appropriate ways to express its faith through a process of inculturation.

Biblical interpretation needs to integrate faith and reason carefully. The Reformation enshrined the principle *sola scriptura* but, as post-Enlightenment Western culture developed in a more critical, rationalist direction, conservative Protestants and some Catholics turned to a fundamentalist, biblical literalism that continues into our own time. Much of that was changed by the Second Vatican Council. Contemporary Catholic theology has continued to develop, moving beyond an earlier approach that reduced God's revelation to propositions as though in a catechism or collection of historical or scientific truths.

Epilogue

Today, Catholic theology is in dialogue with culture and experience; it is increasingly interdisciplinary, contextual, and pluralistic. Nor have Catholic scholars and scientists been reluctant to engage in the scientific community's work and research. The list of those who have done so is long and distinguished.

The fact that some young Catholics fall into the trap of seeing faith and reason as contrary to each other shows the importance of some basic theological education. Without it one's education remains incomplete and overly specialized, confining students to a narrow epistemology that limits knowledge to what is scientifically demonstrable or to what they learn from social media. Intelligence is one of God's gifts; it brings a critical dimension to our knowing.

12. Christianity does not begin with doctrine but with an experience of grace. Those who encountered Jesus were changed by the experience. They experienced love, forgiveness, and a new sense of freedom. The transcendent God is not absent from our experience, but we need to learn how to recognize the divine presence. God's power and majesty are reflected in nature, and God speaks to us in the quiet of our hearts. We need to be attentive to our deeper desires to discern how God moves our spirits.

To be "in Christ" is to be in his body, the church. St. Paul is clear about this. We are baptized into one body, made one in the Eucharist. The Church makes the risen Jesus visible in its preaching, its ministry, and its worship. We hear the voice of Jesus in the Gospels, and it is challenging. We encounter him in the community of his disciples, in the Scriptures, and in the sacraments that mediate his presence. The Spirit awakens our faith and enables us also to call out "Abba, Father." It transforms our own spirits, making them gentle and loving and giving us gifts for service in Jesus's name.

The Spirit is present in all the faithful, not just the hierarchy, enabling us to see the face of Jesus in the poor, the hungry, and the vulnerable. It is regrettable that so many young Catholics, often concerned about social issues and being generous toward others, remain ignorant of the Church's rich social teaching. They live in an age with the crushing poverty of so many, with so much injustice, violence and war, and so many innocent sufferers. Catholic social teaching has much to offer in addressing these problems.

13. Today, many find the Church unnecessary. Its sins are often more evident than the grace it mediates. They see it as just another institution, too judgmental. The church does not seem to speak to their experience. So, they disaffiliate, join the "nones." They want the Church to welcome those in the LGBTQ community and more adequately recognize the gifts of women. Pope Francis has worked to make the Church a more inclusive, welcoming community, speaking of the Church as a field hospital. He has made efforts to give women a greater role, enabling laypeople, including women, to participate in the Synod of Bishops as voting members, as we have seen. The 2023 Declaration of the Dicastery for the Doctrine of the Faith, *Fiducia Supplicans*, allowing priests to bless individuals in same-sex relationships, is another step in that direction.

We cannot be Christians in isolation from others, however. Christianity is a social reality. We can't fully realize our humanity without companionship and society. A highly individualistic culture erases any sense of social solidarity. As Pope Francis says in his 2020 encyclical *Fratelli Tutti*, "In today's world, the sense of belonging to a single human family is fading, and the dream of working together for justice and peace seems an outdated utopia" (no. 30). The Eucharist unites us with Christ and with one another. As the Body of Christ, the Church makes Christ present to the world, visible in its proclamation, worship, and ministry.

14. If many young people are disconnected from their churches today, that does not mean that they are without genuine Christian values. They respect those who are different and support their inclusion in society and church, especially racial, ethnic, and sexual minorities. Many are open to other religious traditions and willing to learn from them. They are much more concerned about environmental change than their elders. They are willing to serve these val-

ues and if they join a small community, it is often because it has a clear social mission. One study reported that "the top reasons why dechurched mainliners and Catholics would be willing to return to the church have a lot to do with the way the church interacts with the world. In particular, they have an interest in doing tangible good in the community."[15]

A massive study involving five universities, coordinated by Bath University in England, reports that nearly 60 percent of the young people surveyed said they felt very worried by climate change.[16] As Cecilia Gonzalez Andrieu suggests, however, few Catholic parishes address this issue. She argues that the Holy Spirit's work in the world is to orient and nurture creation continually toward the God of life and beauty. Yet, she says "we know ourselves capable of betraying all God has made in ways our ancestors could never imagine. Our Sacred Scriptures do not know human beings will pour deadly sludge into the seas and poison our air. Our early church did not know we would crack the mystery of the atom and build the deadliest weapon imaginable."[17]

Also playing a significant role in disaffiliation are the politics of the culture wars, moving most white evangelicals and even some white Catholics to the right-wing. In an article showing young evangelicals fleeing their churches, William Trollinger writes "that the Christian Right is not about personal morality and Christian/religious values but is instead about a particular right-wing politics—a politics in keeping with the history of fundamentalism—involving white nationalism, hostility to immigrants, unfettered capitalism (which includes a disinterest, at least, in global warming), and intense homophobia."[18]

Being Christian does not mean being a political right-winger. What so many of what those on the extreme right call "family values" are contrary to what many young adults value today, and indeed to the values embodied in the Catholic tradition. They reject the politics of exclusion. Much of the criticism of Pope Francis is based on his failure to invest in the culture wars. He has instead tried to present a more welcoming face to the church, a church "that knows how to open her arms and welcome everyone."[19] Young adults have much to teach us about those who are different. A church that is judgmental and unwelcoming of others will not attract them. The church needs to hear their concerns.

15. The Catholic Church in the 1980s was more open to the social dimensions of its mission. Its bishops developed two pastoral letters addressing important issues, one on peace and the threat of nuclear weapons, another on the economy. The process was widely consultative, calling on scholars and experts from the academy, the military, and science as well as the bishops themselves, and several drafts were published to incorporate critical response to each. Rome, however, was not supportive of the process; in the view of the Vatican, the role of bishops was simply to teach.

The first letter, *The Challenge of Peace and Our Response* (1983), argued that no defensive strategy, nuclear or conventional, which exceeds the limits of proportionality is morally permissible. The letter was widely praised and resulted in similar statements from other churches. The second letter, *Economic Justice for All: Pastoral Letter on Catholic Social Teaching and the U.S. Economy* (1986), was less successful. It stressed that economic choices and institutions must be judged by how they protect or undermine the life and dignity of the human person, support the family, and serve the common good. Catholics in the United States had much more difficulty in accepting this letter, but in many ways it was prophetic. But that was almost forty years ago.

An effort to write a third letter on women was ultimately abandoned after several interventions on the part of the Vatican. Today, the U.S. bishops have focused almost exclusively on abortion, their "preeminent priority," and to a lesser extent on same-sex marriage, despite the attempts of some bishops to broaden their concerns. This approach does little to address adequately the issues many young Catholics are most concerned about. They are not necessarily in favor of abortion, but their concerns are broader. Pope Francis's emphasis on synodality is designed to bring more voices, not just clerical ones, into the church's decision-making processes. The U.S. bishops have been slow to address his concerns.

16. Some speak of our present era as marking the end of Christendom, an era that began in the fourth century when Christianity became the official religion of the Roman Empire and continued as the dominant religion in the West.[20] Pope Francis may be referring to something similar when he speaks of epochal change:

> In our time humanity is experiencing a turning-point in its history, as we can see from the advances being made in so many fields. We can only praise the steps being taken to improve people's welfare in areas such as health care, education and communications. At the same time we have to remember that the majority of our contemporaries are barely living from day to day, with dire consequences. A number of diseases are spreading. The hearts of many people are gripped by fear and desperation, even in the so-called rich countries. The joy of living frequently fades, lack of respect for others and violence are on the rise, and inequality is increasingly evident. It is a struggle to live and, often, to live with precious little dignity (EG 52).

It may be that young people are developing a new kind of faith. They still have spiritual needs, and some find alternative ways and communities to sustain them. Many are eager to help others. James Heft finds a good number of nonaffiliated young adults who still believe in God and pray, but he says that without engagement with a religious tradition, that religious sensitivity will not endure in a secular and commercialized culture.[21] Once again, what they need most is not a doctrinal approach or the *Catechism*, but warm and welcoming communities that share their social concerns.

17. Catholic symbols also are powerful; they speak not just to our head but to our affective nature. They move our hearts. Think of

those images of Pope Francis praying alone in the darkness and rain before St. Peter's at the beginning of the pandemic in 2020, or of the Masses celebrated on the Mexican side of the border before the intimidating walls excluding migrants. The Eucharist itself can be a powerful symbol.

The Second Vatican Council called all the faithful "to that full, conscious, and active participation in liturgical celebrations that is demanded by the very nature of the liturgy" (SC 14), but this means more than just taking on some ministerial role in the liturgy. It means uniting with Christ's offering himself to the Father for the salvation of the world. There is a cosmic dimension to liturgy. As Louis Cameli writes:

> Each time we celebrate the Eucharist, the stakes are high. With our world and our human family, we struggle before the enigma of sin constituted by both our personal failures and the world's brokenness. We struggle before the enigma of death that seems to signal our extinction and the utter futility of our lives. When we participate in the Eucharist, when we engage and join the mystery of the one who dies and rises and is victor over sin and death, we worship with him in spirit and in truth and join in his victory.[22]

18. If the doctrine of salvation is fundamental to Christianity, conservative Christians have too often impoverished it, reducing it to a narrow concept of "getting saved" and going to heaven, rooted in Anselm's theology of substitutionary atonement. His theology has been virtually canonized by evangelical Christianity, made one of its five fundamentals. Catholic piety and liturgy have been shaped by it also.

Yet the biblical sense for salvation in both testaments is much richer. God's salvation, revealed in Jesus's preaching of the kingdom of God, sees God's salvific grace transforming us now and creation itself, setting both free from corruption in the world to come. The good news of God's reign needs to be translated anew for every age and generation. It is not distant, but present among us, to free us from our sins, challenge oppressive structures, and bring us into communion with God and one another.

We ourselves can mediate God's grace to others when we act toward them with compassion and love. Grace is always saving and transforming. Few better illustrate the power of God's unconditional love than Father Greg Boyle in his stories about the troubled young people who come to Homeboy Industries, where they experience acceptance and love.[23] Clint Eastwood's film *Gran Torino* beautifully demonstrates how a lonely and racist old man is transformed by the warmth of his Hmong neighbors, including a troubled teenage boy for whom he gradually becomes a surrogate father figure and his sister, a lovely girl who befriends him.

God's saving work is not done. God continues to work through the evolutionary process, not by controlling or intervening to accomplish the divine purpose but in undiscoverable ways drawing all creation to himself through the life-giving Spirit. Jesus himself, the Father's beloved Son, is the Alpha and the Omega, the beginning and the end of God's salvific work, drawing all creation to its fulfillment when God will be all in all.

19. The present state of our world is discouraging to many. As we have argued, we live in society where truth is no longer honored; it is frequently ignored in our political dialogue, which has become increasingly cynical, angry, and aggressive. Our education is no longer informed by the great humanistic tradition of the West that emphasized human rights, rooted in the dignity of the person created in the image of God and the transcendental values of unity, truth, goodness, and beauty. A pervasive secularity is skeptical if not dismissive of any vision beyond the material.

Religion has not disappeared; it continues as a strong cultural force in the global South but frequently leads to violence between peoples and creeds, making interreligious dialogue increasingly important. However, in the West—for those still religious—religion has been largely reduced to the private and the subjective, or to culturally determined fundamentalist traditions, but there is another side to the story.

20. Today, an increasing number of psychologists and social scientists are commenting on the positive dimensions of faith and religious belonging. We long for something to give meaning to our lives. Young people need the example of their parents, supporting communities, and a culture able to look beyond the immediate and the material. They need to discover again the God who loves them, the God for whom their hearts long.

I think again of the young woman I mentioned at the beginning of this book who regretted having learned nothing about religion from those closest to her. We owe these young people so much more.

Notes

Introduction

1. Michael J. O'Loughlin, "Most young Catholics say they are spiritual or religious. That doesn't mean you'll find them at Mass," *America* online, February 24, 2022; based on Springtime Research Institute, "The State of Religion & Young People 2021, Catholic Edition: Navigating Uncertainty."

2. Heidi Glenn, "Losing Our Religion: The Growth of the 'Nones,'" National Public Radio, January 2019.

3. Ronald Rolheiser, *The Holy Longing: The Search for a Christian Spirituality* (New York: Doubleday, 1999).

4. Thomas P. Rausch, *Holy Blasphemies: God, Mystery, and the Spiritual* (Mahwah, NJ: Paulist Press, 2023).

Chapter 1

1. Pew Research Center, "In U.S., Decline of Christianity Continues at Rapid Pace," October 17, 2019.

2. Pew Research Center, "Among U.S. Latinos, Catholicism Continues to Decline but Is Still the Largest Faith," April 13, 2023.

3. Michael J. O'Loughlin, "Survey: Mass attendance drops after Covid, but U.S. Catholics are hopeful for their church," *America* online May 16, 2023.

4. Bryan T. Froehle and Mary L. Gautier, *Catholicism in the USA: A Portrait of the Catholic Church in the United States* (Maryknoll, NY: Orbis Books, 2000), 23.

5. Christian Smith and Melinda Lundquist Denton, *Soul Searching: The Religious and Spiritual Lives of American Teenagers* (New York: Oxford University Press, 2005), 194. See Thomas P. Rausch, *Being Catholic in a Culture of Choice* (Collegeville, MN: Liturgical Press, 2006), 3–9.

6. Daniel A. Cox, "Generation Z and the Future of Faith in America," Survey Center on American Life, March 24, 2022.

7. Pew Research Center, "Among U.S. Latinos, Catholicism Continues to Decline."

8. Allan Figueroa Deck, "New Pastoral-Theological Directions on Faith, Spirituality, and Leadership Formation of Hispanic/Latinx Youth and Young Adults in Light of CARA's Research," in *Faith and Spiritual Life of Young Adult Catholics in a Rising Hispanic Church*, ed. Thomas P. Gaunt (Collegeville, MN: Liturgical Press, 2022), 73–81 at 75.

9. Robert David Sullivan, "Survey: A third of young Catholics expect to attend Mass less often after the Pandemic," *America*, November 10, 2021.

10. Jean M. Twenge, *iGen: Why Today's Super-Connected Kids Are Growing Up Less Rebellious, More Tolerant, Less Happy—and Completely Unprepared for Adulthood* (New York: Atria Books, 2017), 127–30. Twenge uses iGen ("i" as in iPhone, among other descriptors) for Generation Z; see 2–7.

11. James L. Heft, "Understanding and Responding to Non-Affiliation," in *Empty Churches: Non-affiliation in America*, ed. James L. Heft and Jan E. Stets (New York: Oxford University Press, 2021), 337.

12. Carol Ann MacGregor and Ashlyn Haycook, "Lapsed Catholics and Other Religious Non-affiliates," in Heft and Stets, *Empty Churches*, 91.

13. Jan E. Stets, "Introduction," in Heft and Stets, *Empty Churches*, 18–19.

14. Robert J. McCarty and John M. Vitek, *Going, Going, Gone: The Dynamics of Disaffiliation in Young Catholics* (Winona, MN: Saint Mary's Press, 2017), 13–24.

15. See David Gushee, "The problem with white evangelicalism is not Jesus," *Faith & Leadership*, October 27, 2020.

16. Jim Davis and Michael Graham with Ryan P. Burge, *The Great Dechurching* (Grand Rapids, MI: Zondervan, 2023), 111.

17. Brett C. Hoover, "The Rise of Religious Disaffiliation: Political Tribalism and Waning Religiosity," *Commonweal* online, April 27, 2023.

18. See Rausch, *Being Catholic*, 16–17.

19. Phil Davignon, *Church Life Journal*, "Misunderstanding the Rise of the Nones," September 16, 2022; see James K. A. Smith, *Desiring the Kingdom: Worship, Worldview, and Cultural Formation* (Grand Rapids, MI: Baker Academic, 2009), 39–63.

20. Cox, "Generation Z and the Future of Faith in America."

21. Smith and Denton, *Soul Searching*, 261.

22. Twenge, *iGen*, 134.

23. Wade Clark Roof, *Spiritual Marketplace: Baby Boomers and the Remaking of Religion* (Princeton, NJ: Princeton University Press, 1999).

24. Robert Neelly Bellah, "Religion and the Shape of National Culture," *America* 181, no. 3 (1999): 10.

25. Scot McKnight, "Jesus vs. Paul," *Christianity Today*, December 3, 2010; Michael Gerson, "Trump should fill Christians with rage. How come he doesn't?," *Washington Post*, September 1, 2022.

26. Stephen Bullivant, *Nonverts: The Making of Ex-Christian America* (New York: Oxford University Press, 2022), 124–27 at 123.

27. Smith and Denton, *Soul Searching*, 162–63.

28. Christian Smith, "Moralistic Therapeutic Deism," in *Passing on the Faith: Transforming Traditions for the Next Generations of Jews, Christians, and Muslims*, ed. James L. Heft (New York: Fordham University Press, 2006), 64–65.

29. Robert D. Putnam, "Bowling Alone: America's Declining Social Capital," *Journal of Democracy* 6, no. 1 (1995); *Bowling Alone: The Collapse and Revival of American Community* (New York: Simon & Schuster, 2000).

30. Putnam, *Bowling Alone*, 25.

31. Putnam, *Bowling Alone*, 67.

32. David E. Campbell, "Non-religiosity, Secularism, and Civil Society," in Heft and Stets, *Empty Churches*, 224.

33. Robert Wuthnow, *Loose Connections: Joining Together in America's Fragmented Communities* (Cambridge, MA: Harvard University Press, 1998), 218.

34. See Hosffman Ospino, "US Young Adult Catholics Discerning Spirituality and Family Life: What Is the Verdict?" in Gaunt, *Faith and Spiritual Life of Young Adult Catholics*, 63–64.

35. Pew Research Center, "Teens, Social Media and Technology 2022."

36. Pew Research Center, "Teens, Social Media and Technology 2022."

37. Twenge, *iGen*, 51.

38. Jean Twenge, *iGen*, 231–33.

39. Roy Pereira, *Uniting Mind, Body, Spirit: Science and the Spiritual Exercises of St. Ignatius* (Mahwah, NJ: Paulist Press, 2024).

40. Nicholas Kardaras, *Glow Kids: How Screen Addiction Is Hijacking Our Kids—and How to Break the Trance* (New York: St. Martin's Press, 2016), 11–19 at 18.

41. Jean Twenge, *iGen*, 71–75.

42. Jean Twenge, *iGen*, 176.

43. Pope Francis, "An Address to Young People during the Synod," in *L'Osservatore Romano*, October 8–9, 2018, 7.

44. Derek Thompson, "Why American Teens Are so Sad," *The Atlantic*, April 11, 2022.

45. Susie Demarinis, "Loneliness at epidemic levels in America," *PubMed Central*, January 28, 2020).

46. CDC, Youth Risk Behavior Survey, 2020–2021.

47. Daniel Cox, "Growing Up Lonely: Generation Z," *Institute for Family Studies*, April 6, 2022.

48. Twenge, *iGen*, 109.

49. Ryan Jenkins, "3 Things Making Gen Z the Loneliest Generation," *Psychology Today*, August 16, 2022.

50. Charles Taylor, *A Secular Age* (Cambridge, MA: The Belknap Press of Harvard University, 2007), 70.

51. Jean Twenge, *iGen*, 139.

Notes

52. See Tara Isabella Burton, *Strange Rites: New Religions for a Godless World* (New York: Public Affairs, 2020).

Chapter 2

1. Moisés Naím, *The Revenge of Power: How Autocrats Are Reinventing Politics for the 21st Century* (New York: St. Martin's Press, 2022), 158.
2. Ralph Keyes, *The Post-Truth Era: Dishonesty and Deception in Contemporary Life* (New York: St. Martin's Press, 2004), 148.
3. José Luis Narvaja, "Benedict XVI and Relativism in the Life of the Church," *La Civiltà Cattolica*, June 15, 2017.
4. Keyes, *The Post-Truth Era*, 5.
5. Keys, *The Post-Truth Era*, chapter 8, "Mentors and Role Models."
6. Keyes, *The Post-Truth Era*, 132–35.
7. Keyes, *The Post-Truth Era*, 124–28, 183.
8. Jane Mayer, "Donald Trump's Ghostwriter Tells All," *New Yorker*, July 18, 2016
9. Tony Rehagen, "Welcome to Post-Truth America," *Boston College Magazine*, Summer 2020.
10. Mark Edmundson, "Truth Takes a Vacation: Trumpism and the American Philosophical Tradition," *Harper's Magazine*, January 2023, 40–41.
11. Moisés Naím, *The Revenge of Power*, 70–88.
12. Adolfo Nicolás, "Challenges to Jesuit Higher Education Today," *Conversations on Jesuit Higher Education* 40 (2011).
13. Ruth Igielnik, Scott Keeter, and Hannah Hartig, "Behind Biden's 2020 Victory," Pew Research Center, June 30, 2021.
14. Public Religion Research Institute, "Challenges in Moving toward a More Inclusive Democracy: Findings from the 2022 American Values Survey," December 27, 2022.
15. Sarah Eekhoff Zylstra, "Praise the Lord and Pass the Ammunition," *Christianity Today*, July 24, 2017.
16. Stella Rouse and Shibley Telhami, "Most Republicans Support Declaring the United States a Christian Nation," *Politico*,

September 21, 2022; see also Thomas P. Rausch, "Trump, the 'religious right' and white Christian nationalism," *America* online, January 5, 2024.

17. Robert P. Jones, *The Hidden Roots of White Supremacy and the Path to a Shared American Future* (New York: Simon & Schuster, 2023), 299; see also Pamela Cooper White, *The Psychology of Christian Nationalism* (Minneapolis: Fortress Press, 2022).

18. Matteo Wong, "We Haven't Seen the Worst of Fake News," *Atlantic*, December 20, 2022.

19. Andrew S. Weiss, "Vladimir Putin's Political Meddling Revives Old KGB Tactics," *Wall Street Journal*, February 17, 2017.

20. Office of Public Affairs, United States Department of Justice, "Grand Jury Indicts 12 Russian Intelligence Officers for Hacking Offenses Related to the 2016 Election," July 13, 2018.

21. Elizabeth Thompson, Katie Nicholson, Jason Ho, "COVID-19 disinformation being spread by Russia, China, say experts," CBNC News, May 26, 2020.

22. Roger Haight, *The Nature of Theology: Challenges, Frameworks, Basic Beliefs* (Maryknoll, NY: Orbis Books, 2022), 8.

23. Pope Francis, *Laudato Si'*, no. 122.

24. See Charles Taylor, *A Secular Age* (Cambridge, MA: The Belknap Press of Harvard University, 2007).

25. John F. Haught, *God and the New Atheism: A Critical Response to Dawkins, Harris, and Hitchens* (Louisville, KY: Westminster John Knox Press, 2008), xi.

26. Pope Benedict XVI, *Jesus of Nazareth*, part 1 (New York: Doubleday, 2007), 92.

27. See Karl Rahner, *Foundations of Christian Faith* (New York: Crossroad, 1982), 31–34, 51–53; first German edition 1976.

28. See Rachel Lu, "The Comfort of Philosophy: What the church can give to the world in a time of anxiety and doubt," *America*, February 2023, 30–35, 41.

29. David Brooks, "How America Got Mean," *Atlantic*, September 2023, 73.

30. Nathan Hiller, "The End of the English Major," *New Yorker*, March 6, 2023, 28.

31. Shelby Kearns, "Our religious studies programs are in trouble. Here's what we miss out on if we don't save them," *America* online, April 15, 2021.

32. Greg Lukianoff and Jonathan Haidt, "The Coddling of the American Mind" *Atlantic* 136, no. 2 (2015): 45; see also Jean M. Twenge, *iGen: Why Today's Super-Connected Kids Are Growing Up Less Rebellious, More Tolerant, Less Happy—and Completely Unprepared for Adulthood* (New York: Atria Books, 2017), 249–58.

33. *Summa Theologiae*, I,84,5.

34. Scott and Kimberly Hahn, *Rome Sweet Home: Our Journey to Catholicism* (San Francisco: Ignatius Press, 1993).

Chapter 3

1. William D. Dinges, "Our teens are leaving the church. Why?," *America* online, August 28, 2018.

2. Joseph Ratzinger, *Truth and Tolerance: Christian Belief and World Religions* (San Francisco: Ignatius Press, 2004), 252.

3. Sandra Schneiders, *The Revelatory Text: Interpreting the New Testament as Sacred Scripture* (Collegeville, MN: Liturgical Press, 1999), 22–23; see also Brevard S. Childs, *Biblical Theology in Crisis* (Philadelphia: The Westminster Press, 1970).

4. John Paul II, *Message to the Pontifical Academy of Scientists*, no 4.

5. Avery Dulles, *Models of Revelation* (Garden City, NY: Doubleday, 1985), 39.

6. Dulles, *Models*, 44.

7. Sallie McFague, *Models of God: Theology for an Ecological, Nuclear Age* (Philadelphia: Fortress Press, 1987).

8. Annie Dillard, *For the Time Being* (New York: Alfred A. Knopf, 1999), 167–68.

9. Christian Smith, "Moralistic Therapeutic Deism," in *Passing on the Faith: Transforming Traditions of the Next Generation of Jews, Christians, and Muslims*, ed. James L. Heft (New York: Fordham University Press, 2006), 65.

10. See Massimo Borghesi, *Catholic Discordance: Neoconservatism vs. the Field Hospital Church of Pope Francis* (Collegeville, MN: Liturgical Press, 2021).

11. See Thomas P. Rausch, "Does Doctrine Change," *America* online, November 30, 2015; also "Doctrine: At the Service of the Pastoral Mission of the Church," *La Civiltà Cattolica*, July 21, 2017.

12. International Theological Commission, "*Sensus Fidei* in the Life of the Church," 2014.

13. See David Gibson, "Sin is the failure to bother to love: A history of Catholic ethics and morality," *America* online, February 3, 2023.

Chapter 4

1. Edward Schillebeeckx, *Interim Report on the Books Jesus & Christ* (New York: Crossroad, 1982), 7–10 at 10.

2. Pontifical Council for the Promotion of the New Evangelization, *Directory for Catechesis* (Washington, DC: United States Conference of Catholic Bishops, 2020), no. 29.

3. See John L. Allen, "Book indicates pope is a moderate realist," *National Catholic Reporter*, April 19, 2013.

4. See Michael Downey, *Altogether Gift: A Trinitarian Spirituality* (Maryknoll, NY: Orbis Books, 2000), 48–55.

5. Joseph Ratzinger/Benedict XVI, *Teaching and Learning the Love of God: Being a Priest Today* (San Francisco: Ignatius Press, 2016), 292.

6. Karl Rahner, *Foundations of Christian Faith: An Introduction to the Idea of Christianity* (New York: Seabury Press, 1978), 53.

7. *Summa Theologiae*, I.84.5.

8. Elizabeth A. Johnson, "The Earth's Beloved Community," *America*, June 2023, 26–27.

9. Roger Haight, *The Nature of Theology* (Maryknoll, NY: Orbis Books, 2022), 110.

10. *Spiritual Exercises*, nos. 235–36.

11. Augustine, *Confessions*, 10, 27.

12. See Alexander Heidel, *The Babylonian Genesis: The Story of Creation* (Chicago: University of Chicago Press, 1951).

Notes

13. Thomas Merton, *New Seeds of Contemplation* (New York: New Directions, 1961), 228–29.

14. Gerhard Lohfink, *Jesus of Nazareth: What He Wanted, Who He Was* (Collegeville, MN: Liturgical Press, 2012), 274 (b. Sotah, 47a).

15. Elizabeth Johnson, *Consider Jesus: Waves of Renewal in Christology* (New York: Crossroad, 1990), 50.

16. Baptism of Jesus, Wedding at Cana, Proclaiming the Kingdom, Transfiguration, Institution of the Eucharist.

17. Eamonn Bredin, *Rediscovering Jesus: Challenge of Discipleship* (Quezon City, Philippines: Claretian Publications, 1986), 40.

18. See Rudolph Bultmann, *The History of the Synoptic Tradition* (Oxford: Blackwell,1963), 102–4.

19. Brian E. Daley, "The Unexpected God: How Christian Faith Discovers the Holy Spirit," Duquesne University 7th Annual Holy Spirit Lecture and Colloquium, September 23, 2011.

20. See Richard R. Gaillardetz, "Synodality and the Francis Pontificate: A Fresh Reception of Vatican II," *Theological Studies* 84, no. 1 (2023): 44–60.

21. See the document of the International Theological Commission, "*Sensus Fidei* in the Life of the Church," nos. 72–73.

22. Beata Pastwa-Wojciechowska, Iwona Grzegorzewska, and Mirella Wojciechowska, "The Role of Religious Values and Beliefs in Shaping Mental Health and Disorders," *Religions* 12, no. 840 (2021): 2.

23. Pastwa-Wojciechowska et al., "The Role of Religious Values," 7–8.

24. Sam A. Hardy and Gregory S. Longo, "Developmental Perspectives of Youth Non-affiliation," in *Empty Churches: Non-affiliation in America*, ed. James L. Heft and Jan E. Stets (New York: Oxford University Press, 2021), 145.

Chapter 5

1. Christian Smith and Melinda Lundquist Denton, *Soul Searching: The Religious and Spiritual Lives of American Teenagers* (New York: Oxford University Press, 2005), 143–44.

2. Scot McKnight, "Jesus vs. Paul," *Christianity Today*, December 3, 2010.

3. Michael Gerson, "Trump should fill Christians with rage. How come he doesn't?," *Washington Post*, September 1, 2022.

4. This is often illustrated in art as the "Peaceful Kingdom."

5. Bredin, *Rediscovering Jesus*, 25.

6. Elizabeth Johnson, *Consider Jesus: Waves of Renewal in Christology* (New York: Crossroad, 1990), 54.

7. Pontifical Council for the Promotion of the New Evangelization, *Directory for Catechesis* (Washington, DC: United States Conference of Catholic Bishops, 2020), no. 30.

8. Roger Haight, *The Nature of Theology* (Maryknoll, NY: Orbis Books, 2022), 72.

9. Karl Rahner, *Foundations of Christian Faith: An Introduction to the Idea of Christianity* (New York: Crossroad, 1982), 113; first published in German, 1976.

10. Pope Francis, *Laudato Si'*, no. 240.

11. Terrence Tilley, *The Disciples' Jesus: Christology as Reconciling Practice* (Maryknoll, NY: Orbis Books, 2008), 244–48.

12. Edward Schillebeeckx, *Jesus: An Experiment in Christology* (New York: Seabury Press, 1979), 153.

13. Albert Nolan, *Jesus before Christianity* (Maryknoll, NY: Orbis Books, 1978), 84.

14. See Michael Downey, *The Depth of God's Reach: A Spirituality of Christ's Descent* (Maryknoll, NY: Orbis Books, 2018).

15. Walter Kasper, *Jesus the Christ* (New York: Paulist Press, 1976), 152.

16. Johnson, *Consider Jesus*, 75.

17. Elizabeth A. Johnson, *Quest for the Living God: Mapping Frontiers in the Theology of God* (New York: Continuum 2007), 193.

18. Quoted in James Martin, "Does the Holy Spirit Choose the Pope," *Time*, March 11, 2013.

19. John Paul II, *Crossing the Threshold of Hope*, ed. Vittorio Messori (New York: Random House, 1994), 61.

20. John F. Haught, *Making Sense of Evolution: Darwin, God, and the Drama of Life* (Louisville, KY: Westminster John Knox, 2020).

21. See John F. Haught, "Love, Hope, and the Cosmic Future," Center for Christogenesis, January 16, 2017.

22. Ilia Delio, *Christ in Evolution* (Maryknoll, NY: Orbis Books, 2008), 132.

23. Jürgen Moltmann, *God in Creation* (San Francisco: Harper & Row, 1985), 88.

24. John F. Haught, *God after Darwin: A Theology of Evolution* (Boulder, CO: Westview Press, 2008), 58; see also Elizabeth A. Johnson, *Ask the Beasts: Darwin and the God of Love* (London: Bloomsbury, 2014), 158.

25. Edward Schillebeeckx, *Church: The Human Story of God* (New York: Crossroad, 1990), 90.

26. Alfred North Whitehead, *Process and Reality: An Essay in Cosmology* (New York: Free Press, 178), 351.

27. Daniel J. Harrington, "Law and the Giver of Life: John P. Meier revisits the historical Jesus," *America* online, October 19, 2009.

28. For the following, see Larry W. Hurtado, *Lord Jesus Christ: Devotion to Jesus in Earliest Christianity* (Grand Rapids, MI: William B. Eerdmans, 2003).

29. Jürgen Moltmann, *The Coming of Christ: Christian Eschatology* (Minneapolis: Fortress, 1996), xv.

30. See Thomas P. Rausch, *Eschatology, Liturgy, and Christology* (Collegeville, MN: Liturgical Press, 2012).

31. David Bentley Hart, *That All Shall Be Saved: Heaven, Hell, & Universal Salvation* (New Haven, CT: Yale University Press, 2019).

Epilogue

1. Pope Francis cites Benedict XVI, who said, "Being a Christian is not the result of an ethical choice or a lofty idea, but the encounter with an event, a person, which gives life a new horizon and a decisive direction"; *Evangelii Gaudium*, no. 7.

2. J. D. Long-Garcia, "Latino Catholics are leaving the Church. Can we welcome them back?," *America* online, June 29, 2023; see also Pew Research Center, "Among U.S. Latinos, Catholicism Continues to Decline but Is Still the Largest Faith," April 13, 2023.

3. See Tara Isabella Burton, *Strange Rites: New Religions for a Godless World* (New York: Public Affairs, 2020).

4. Mark M. Gray, Michael J. Kramarek, and Thomas P. Gaunt, "Faith and Spiritual Life of Catholics in the United States (the Pandemic)," report, Center for Applied Research in the Apostolate, Washington, DC, 2021, 70.

5. Gregory Boyle, *Barking to the Choir: The Power of Radical Kinship* (New York: Simon & Schuster, 2017), 26–27.

6. See Richard T. Hughes, *Christian America and the Kingdom of God* (Urbana: University of Illinois Press, 2009); see also Michael Gerson, "Trump should fill Christians with rage: How come he doesn't?," *Washington Post*, September 1, 2022.

7. Allan Figueroa Deck, "New Pastoral-Theological Directions on Faith, Spirituality, and Leadership Formation of Hispanic/Latinx Youth and Young Adults in Light of CARA's Research" in *Faith and Spiritual Life of Young Adult Catholics in a Rising Hispanic Church*, ed. Thomas P. Gaunt (Collegeville, MN: Liturgical Press, 2022), 82.

8. XVI Ordinary General Assembly of the Synod of Bishops, *Instrumentum Laboris* for the First Session (October 2023).

9. Thomas Reese, "Cardinal Hollerich guides the synod with a gentle hand," Religious News Service online, October 20, 2023.

10. Christian Smith, with Kyle Longest, Jonathan Hill, and Kari Christoffersen, *Young Catholic America: Emerging Adults in, out of, and Gone from the Church* (New York: Oxford University Press, 2014), 272–73.

11. Hosffman Ospino, "US Young Adult Catholics Discerning Spirituality and Family Life: What Is the Verdict?," in Gaunt, *Faith and Spiritual Life of Young Adult Catholics*, 60.

12. Hosffman Ospino, "US Young Adult Catholics," 67.

13. See Massimo Faggioli, "The great displacement of theology. Where is the future of 'faith seeking understanding'?" *LaCroix International*, August 17, 2023.

14. See Massimo Faggioli, "A Wake-Up Call to Liberal Theologians: Academic Theology Needs the Church," *Commonweal*, May 16, 2018.

15. Jim Davis and Michael Graham with Ryan P. Burge, *The Great Dechurching* (Grand Rapids, MI: Zondervan, 2023), 108.

16. Roger Harrabin, "Climate change: Young people very worried—survey," BBC News, September 14, 2021.

17. Cecilia González-Andrieu, "The Catholic Church has the potential to change the world. Are we squandering it?," *America* online, August 17, 2023.

18. William V. Trollinger, "Religious Non-affiliation: Expelled by the Right," in *Empty Churches: Non-affiliation in America*, ed. James L. Heft and Jan E. Stets (New York: Oxford University Press, 2021), 189–90; see also Pamela Cooper-White, *The Psychology of Christian Nationalism* (Minneapolis: Fortress Press, 2022).

19. Pope Francis, "General Audience, October 2, 2013," in *The Church of Mercy: A Vision for the Church* (Chicago: Loyola Press, 2014), 31.

20. See James L. Heft, "Understanding and Responding to Non-affiliation," in Heft and Stets, *Empty Churches*, 329.

21. James Heft, "Understanding and Responding to Non-affiliation," 336–37.

22. Louis J. Cameli, "The bishops are right. We need a national eucharistic revival. But the current plan isn't enough," *America* online, March 21, 2023.

23. Gregory Boyle, *Barking to the Choir*.

Index

abortion, 124
"Address to Young People during the Synod, An," 15
Adorno, Theodor, 42
Amoris Laetitia, 21
Ampère, André-Marie, 59
Andrieu, Cecilia Gonzalez, 123
Anselm, 44, 75, 98–99, 126
Antiochus IV, 95
apocalyptic, 95–96
Aquinas. *See* Thomas Aquinas
Aristotle, 34–35, 37, 40, 44
Arius, 54
atheism, 36
Augustine, 36, 55, 77, 78
autobiography, religious, xi

Barron, Robert, 118
Barth, Karl, 58
Bellah, Robert Neelly, 6–7
Benedict XVI, Pope, 6, 26, 37, 42, 45, 46, 55, 60, 73, 84, 100–101, 102–3, 105, 118
Bible: Catholics, 47–48; and the church, 50, 67; and faith, 47; historical criticism, 48–49; interpretation, 47–49, 120; literalism, 46–48; and myth, 53; salvation, Jewish Scriptures, 93–96; senses, 49–50
Biden, Joseph, 27, 28
Big Lie, 29, 33
body image, 12, 16
Body of Christ, 86–87, 89
Boebert, Lauren, 29
Boniface VIII, Pope, 51
"Bowling Alone," 9
Boyle, Greg, 114, 124
Braille, Louis, 59
Bredin, Eamonn, 82, 97
Brooks, David, 38
Bullivant, Stephen, 7
Bush, George W., 27, 93

Calvin, John, 57
Cameli, Louis, 126
Campbell, David, 10

143

Caritas in Veritate, 101
Cavadini, John, 5
Center for Applied Research in the Apostolate (CARA), 2, 3, 114, 155
Challenge of Peace and Our Response, The, 124
Chenu, Marie-Dominique, 60
Christendom, 125
Christology. *See under* Jesus Christ
Church, 86–89, 121, 122
church fathers, 53–54
Church Life Journal, 5
Cigna, 15–16
Clement of Alexandria, 53, 54
climate change, 123
Clinton, Bill, 27
collegiality, 61
companionship, 18
Congar, Yves, 60
conservatism, 4–5, 126
Consolmagno, Guy J., 59
conspiracy theories, 33
Conway, Kellyanne, 27
Copernicus, Nicholas, 58
Council of Trent, 52
creation, 18, 76–78, 103–7
culture wars, 123–24
Curie, Marie, 59

Daley, Brian, 85
Daniélou, Jean, 60
Darwin, Charles, 51
Dawkins, Richard, 36
de Chardin, Teilhard, 62, 105
Deck, Allan, 3

Dei Verbum, 47, 52, 67
Delio, Ilia, 103, 105, 106
de Lubac, Henri, 61
Denton, Melinda Lundquist, 2, 6, 8, 58
dependency shift, 17–18
depression, 17
Derrida, Jacques, 26
DeSantis, Ron, 29
Descartes, René, 24
Deus Caritas Est, 6
Dillard, Annie, 58
Directory for Catechesis, 69–70
disaffiliation, religious, xi–xii, 1–2, 4, 20, 42, 65, 113, 123
disciples, 70–71, 86–87
disinformation, 32–34
diversity, equity, and inclusion (DEI), 120
Divino Afflante Spiritu, 47, 60
doctrine, 65, 69, 88
Dogmatic Constitution on Divine Revelation. See *Dei Verbum*
Dogmatic Constitution on the Church, 98
Drey, Johann Sebastian, 60
Dulles, Avery, 52

Easter Experience, 70–71
Eastwood, Clint, 127
Economic Justice for All: Pastoral Letter on Catholic Social Teaching and the U.S. Economy, 124
economics, 64–65, 124
education, 38–39, 41, 44, 119, 121

Index

Einstein, Albert, 104
Elijah, 73–74
Enlightenment, the, 35
epistemology, 24, 118–19
Eucharist, 126
evangelicalism, 7, 20, 31, 92–93, 114, 115, 123
Evangelii Gaudium, 64–65, 70
evil, 56
evolution, 51–52, 105–6
EWTN, 118
Ex Corde Ecclesiae, 44
exodus, 94
experience, 69–71, 121

Faggioli, Massimo, 119–20
faith: and the Bible, 47; positive effects, 90–91; and reason, 43, 51, 120–21; and theology, 44–45
fall, the, 78
Fides et Ratio, 45, 107
Fiducia Supplicans, 122
Foucault, Michel, 26
Fox News, 28
Francis, Pope, 6, 14–15, 18–19, 21–22, 26–27, 32, 64–66, 70, 88, 89, 90, 101, 111, 113, 115, 122, 123–24, 125, 126
Fratelli Tutti, 15, 18–19, 32, 122
Freud, Sigmund, 25
fundamentalism, 46–48, 57

Galileo, Galilee, 45, 51, 58
Gaudium et Spes, 61
Generation Z, xi–xii, xiii, 3, 17
Genesis, 49, 77–78

Gerson, Michael, 7, 93
God: and creation, 76–77, 103–7; ethical dimension, 74–75, 101; and evil, 55–58; and experience, 72–73; five ways, 36; immanence, 76–77; and the Jews, 94–95; kenosis, 106–7; and knowledge, 35; love, 127; models, 56–57; mystery, 75–76; omnipotence, 105; otherness, 75; presence, 78–79; revelation, 52; salvation, 102–3; and the Spirit, 85; transcendence, 72–74, 101–2
Gospel, 52–53
grace, 101, 103, 110, 126–27
Gran Torino, 127
Greco-Roman world, 53–54
Greene, Marjorie Taylor, 29
Gregory of Nyssa, 75, 112
gun violence, 33–34

Habermas, Jürgen, 46
Hahn, Kimberly, 40
Hahn, Scott, 40
Haidt, Jonathan, 39
Haight, Roger, 35, 76, 101
Harris, Kamala, 29
Harris, Sam, 36
Hart, David Bentley, 112
Haught, John, 36, 103, 105, 106
Heft, James, 4, 91, 125
Hegel, Georg Friedrich Wilhelm, 25
Heisenberg, Werner, 104

higher power, 8
Hildegard of Bingen, 58, 67
Hill, Anita, 27
Hispanic Catholics, 1–2, 114
Hitchens, Christopher, 36
Hollerich, Jean-Claude, 116
Holy Spirit, 85–86, 105
Hoover, Brett, 5
Howard, Philip, 32
Humani Generis, 51
Hurtado, Larry, 108

Ignatius of Loyola, St., 73, 105
illiteracy, 5, 30–32, 114–15
indeterminacy, 104
individualism, 6–7, 8–9, 41, 66, 102, 122
information, 30–31, 32
Instruction on the Historical Truth of the Gospels, 81
Instrumentum Laboris, 115
Isaac of Nineveh, 112

Jesus Christ: Christology, 107–10, 111–12; and Church, 89, 121; death, 98–99; and disciples, 86–87; ethical teacher, 84; and experience, 69–71, 84, 121; and Gospels, 81–82, 109–10; historical, 80–82, 107–8; kenosis, 106–7; kingdom of God, 96–100, 101, 110; Lord (*kyrios*), 108; mystery, 84–85; parables, 81–82; Paul, 108, 109; preexistence, 109; resurrection, 70–72; and revelation, 52; and salvation, 96–99; sayings, 82–83; signs and wonders, 70–72; social dimension of ministry, 100; story, 79–80; table fellowship, 97–98; worship of, 108–9
Jews, 93–96
John Paul II, Pope, 44, 45, 51, 80, 105, 107, 116
Johnson, Elizabeth, 76, 80, 97, 103, 104, 105
Johnson, Mike, 29
John XXIII, John, Pope St., 61
Jones, Robert P., 31
Josephus, 79–80
Justin Martyr, 53–54

Kant, Immanuel, 24
Kardaras, Nicholas, 13
Kasper, Walter, 103
Kaveny, Cathleen, 5
Kennedy, John F., 9
Keyes, Ralph, 26, 27
Kierkegaard, Søren, 24
kingdom of God, 96–103, 110–11
knowledge, 34–38, 40, 42

Laplace, Pierre, 104
Latinos, 3
Laudato Si', 18, 64, 111
Lemaître, Georges, 59
Leo XIII, Pope, 64
LGBTQ community, 65–66, 116–17, 122
liberal arts, 39

Index

liminal nones, 113
liturgy, 126
Lohfink, Gerhard, 80
Lombard, Peter, 38
loneliness, 15–18, 155
loose connections, 10–11
Lukianoff, Greg, 39

Marconi, Guglielmo, 59
Maréchal, Joseph, 60
marriage, 11
Marx, Karl, 25, 100
Maximus the Confessor, 112
McClure, Paul, 8
McFague, Sallie, 57
McKnight, Scot, 93
Meier, John P., 107–8
Melito of Sardis, 49
Mendel, Gregor, 59
Merton, Thomas, 79
messianism, 95
modernity, 24–25, 34, 118
Möhler, Johannes Adam, 60
Moltmann, Jürgen, 110
moral formation, 38
moralistic therapeutic deism, 8
Morning Edition, xii
Moses, 94
Mother Angelica, 118

Náim, Moisés, 24, 30
Neo-Scholasticism, 60
Newman, John Henry, 60
New Testament, 53, 71, 84, 102, 107–8
Nicolás, Adolfo, 31
Nietzsche, Friedrich, 24–25

Nixon, Richard, 27
Nolan, Albert, 102
"nones," 2–4
nonverts, 7

Origen, 54, 112
original sin, 78. *See also* sin
Ospino, Hosffman, 118
overstimulation, 17

parable of the Good Samaritan, 19
parenting, 6, 91, 114, 116
Passover, 94
Pasteur, Louis, 59
Paul, apostle, 84–86, 87, 102, 106, 108, 109
Pelosi, Nancy, 29, 33
philosophy, 24–25, 53–55
Pius XII, Pope, 47, 51, 60
Plato, 34–35, 67
politics, 19, 27–30, 123
Pontifical Biblical Commission, 47–48, 50, 63, 81
Poorman, Mark, 5
postmodernism, 24–26, 41–42
pre-Socratics, 34
prophets, 95
Protestantism, 6–7, 46, 78
Public Religion Research Institute (PRRI), 31
Putnam, Robert, 9–10

QAnon, 29, 31, 33
quantum mechanics, 104

Rahner, Karl, 37, 60, 75–76, 101
Ratzinger, Joseph. *See* Benedict XVI, Pope
Reagan, Ronald, 27
reason, 43, 51, 120
reign of God. *See* kingdom of God
Rerum Novarum, 64
revelation, 52
Ricci, Matteo, 59
Robertson, Pat, 57–58
Rolheiser, Ronald, xiii
Rousselot, Pierre, 60
Russia, 32

sacraments, 87–88
salvation: and Christ, 96–98; the cross, 98–99; God, 102–3; and grace, 126–27; idea, 92–93; Jewish Scriptures, 93–96; social, 102–3, 111; universal, 112
Santos, George, 29
Schaeffer, Francis, 52
Schillebeeckx, Edward, 69, 84, 102, 107
Schneiders, Sandra, 50
Scholastics, 38
Schwartz, Tony, 28
Science, 35–36, 44–46, 58–59
Scopes, John, 48
Scripture. *See* Bible
Second Vatican Council. *See* Vatican II
secularism, 20, 35–36
sex, 12–13

signs and wonders, 70–72
Simon Peter, 97
sin, 51, 65, 78, 126
skepticism, 24, 26, 34–38
smartphones, 16–17
Smith, Christian, 2, 6, 8, 58, 116
Smith, James K. A., 5
social capital, 9–10
social media, xii, 11–15, 16–17, 27–28, 30–31, 32–33, 117–18
social skills, 14
social teaching, Catholic, 64, 121–22
Spe Salvi, 26, 42, 100–101, 102–3
Spiritual Exercises, 73
Stoeger, Willliam R., 59
Suetonius, 80
suffering, 55–58
suicide, 16
Survey Center on American Life, 6
symbols, Catholic, 125–26
Synod on Synodality, 66, 115–16

Tacitus, 80
Taylor, Charles, 20, 36
Teresa of Calcutta, St., 82
Tertullian, 54
theology: contextual, 62–63; and faith, 43–44; feminist, 63–64; liberation, 62–63; pluralism, 62–66; and science, 44–46

Index

Thomas, apostle, 70
Thomas, Clarence, 27
Thomas Aquinas, 23, 37, 40, 55, 67, 74, 76
3P autocrats, 30
TikTok, 12
Tilley, Terrence, 89, 102
Tracy, David, 62
Trollinger, William, 123
Trump, Donald, 4, 27, 28–29, 32
truth: and Christianity, 23; discovering, 39–40; and politics, 29–30; and postmodernism, 26; post-truth, 23–27, 41; and social media, 27–28; and Trump, 28–29
Twenge, Jean, 3, 12, 14, 16, 20
2020 election, 29, 31

Unam Sanctam, 51
university. *See* education

values, Christian, 113, 115, 122–23
Vatican II, 47, 52, 61–62, 64, 67–68, 100, 126
video games, 13–14

white Christian nationalism, 31–32
Whitehead, Alfred North, 107
Wisdom tradition, 96
Wuthnow, Robert, 10

Xu Guangqi, 59

Youth Risk Behavior Survey, 15–16

www.ingramcontent.com/pod-product-compliance
Lightning Source LLC
Chambersburg PA
CBHW071848230426

43671CB00012B/2106